The Self-Compassion Workbook

THE **Self-Compassion** WORKBOOK

Practical Exercises to Approach Your Thoughts, Emotions, and Actions with Kindness

Joy Johnson, LCSW

ROCKRIDGE
PRESS

For general information on our other products and services or to obtain technical support, please contact our Customer Care Department within the United States at (866) 744-2665, or outside the United States at (510) 253-0500.

Rockridge Press publishes its books in a variety of electronic and print formats. Some content that appears in print may not be available in electronic books, and vice versa.

TRADEMARKS: Rockridge Press and the Rockridge Press logo are trademarks or registered trademarks of Callisto Media Inc. and/or its affiliates, in the United States and other countries, and may not be used without written permission. All other trademarks are the property of their respective owners. Rockridge Press is not associated with any product or vendor mentioned in this book.

Interior and Cover Designer: Erin Yeung
Art Producer: Sara Feinstein
Editor: Crystal Nero
Production Editor: Matthew Burnett
Illustrations © Veris Studio/Creative Market; other illustrations used under license from Shutterstock.com, p. 61.
Author photograph courtesy of Katie Snyder.

ISBN: Print 978-1-64739-806-4
eBook 978-1-64739-481-3
R1

This book is dedicated to those who care for everything and everyone else, but often forget or don't know how to be compassionate with themselves.

Contents

Introduction

Hi, I'm Joy, and I'm a recovering perfectionist. I spent much of my life trying to follow all the rules and do everything right. I'm a natural people pleaser, and I was a good student growing up, which meant I learned that if I did things the "right" way, it would go well for me and I'd avoid conflict. In the process, I used self-criticism to protect myself against suffering. I believed beating myself up would motivate me so I wouldn't become a total failure.

That approach served me well for a time, or so it seemed. I did well academically, eventually becoming a social worker and psychotherapist. However, the more time passed, the more difficult it became to determine the right or perfect thing to do, especially in a field as complex and nuanced as mental health. The rules and systems I had followed so religiously were failing my clients and me and didn't seem to be leading me down the path I expected. I felt exhausted and considered leaving the profession altogether.

To work through the burnout and create a sustainable approach to my work, I had to learn that my belief that I could single-handedly change such a system was unrealistic. My perfectionism was also unhelpful, to myself and my clients. In my one-on-one work with clients, I began to learn that I was meant to simply walk with folks through their pain and struggles, gently reminding them what work was their responsibility and what work was not theirs to carry (such as tending to others' emotions or emotionally taking on the responsibility of changing systemic issues by themselves).

This was a discovery I only could have made through the deep inner work that self-compassion made possible.

What has self-compassion given me? It has allowed me room to breathe and to be myself. It has given me permission to build a life worth living that's my own, rather than one that's based on what everyone else thinks I should do. Self-compassion allows me to be a therapist who partners with my clients on their journey, letting go of the responsibility of trying to remove every roadblock. I can provide support, strategies, tools, plans, referrals, and advocacy, but I don't need to do it all myself. Instead, I can *just be* with my clients. I'm learning to be present for myself and those I love most. I'm still working on it, but my self-critical voice is growing softer and softer.

While writing this book, I've used the very tools laid out here for you. As I began writing, my self-critical voice told me, "You're actually not a great writer. Everyone will see that. How could you think *that* was a good way to put a sentence together? This is too hard for you. You might as well give up now." That voice had kept me from writing in the past, despite the fact that I've always enjoyed and valued it. But now, I have new tools and new ways of moving through that thinking.

I have seen a lot in my 10 years working in mental health. I've worked in psychiatric facilities, 24/7 counseling call centers, outpatient clinics, and clients' homes, and now I run my own private practice. I have yet to meet a client or friend who hasn't been hurt by deeply internalized self-criticism or been helped by learning a little self-compassion.

You may be concerned that self-compassion is silly or fluffy or just not for you. I get that. I've been there and had those thoughts. I was skeptical, too, when I first started to learn about self-compassion. I'm not someone who grew up believing in or even knowing much about things like mindfulness and inner work. But the more I learned and began to use these tools in my daily life, the more I saw their benefits.

The beauty of self-compassion is that you don't have to believe in any of it yet. I simply invite you to try a new way of thinking while reading this book. I invite you to choose your own values and well-being over perfectionism, avoidance, and worries about what other people think. Although self-compassion won't make all your problems go away, it will strengthen your ability to manage day-to-day struggles by helping you learn how to be with and for yourself. In those difficult moments, don't you want to take the emotional load off your shoulders rather than pile more on?

PART ONE

The Value of Self-Compassion

What is self-compassion and why does it matter? Unlike self-esteem, "positive thinking," and other strategies you may have tried before, self-compassion begins with meeting yourself right where you are. We'll explore the foundations of a self-compassion practice, and how this can naturally lead to deeper healing and lasting change.

What Is Self-Compassion?

The simplest way to describe self-compassion is that it's talking to and treating yourself like you would a close friend or loved one. When someone you deeply care about comes to you with a problem or tells you about a mistake they've made, you'll likely offer compassion and caring. You'll try to reassure them and remind them that you love them and don't think they're crazy or a horrible person for the mistake they've made.

Do you give this same treatment to yourself? Do you remind yourself that you are more than this one mistake? Or do you beat yourself up? Do you call yourself names or feel like a failure?

We often struggle to show up for ourselves in the same way we do for others. Sometimes, when I begin discussing self-compassion with people, they think that it feels self-indulgent or silly. But when they pay attention to how they talk to themselves or think about how it would feel for someone to say to them what they're constantly saying to themselves, they can begin to see the potential benefits of more self-compassion.

For example, let's say a coworker you're close to comes to you, distraught, after forgetting half their work presentation. You look at them and scoff, "Wow, I knew it. You're lazy and dumb and you'll never get anywhere—and now every-one knows it. All the work you did on that project is worthless because you'll never get over your fear of public speaking. You might as well quit while you're ahead. I'd say you should never present again. Maybe we should demote you so we can avoid that."

What a horrible friend, right? That's not exactly a supportive response. In our culture, we see kindness to our friends and loved ones as the obvious thing to do. But our own inner self-talk often tends to be more like the critical, unsupportive reaction in our coworker example.

Now let's try on a more compassionate response: You look at your coworker and say softly, "Wow, that sounds tough! I know you worked so hard, and what you prepared was impressive. Most people are afraid of public speaking, and I know you've been under a lot of stress at home lately, too. I'm here for you. Is there anything I can I do to help?"

With this response, you remind your coworker that anxiety about public speaking is normal and that this situation doesn't reflect their true intelligence or ability. You remind them of who they really are, reassure them that this one stumble doesn't define their worth, and let them know you're still there for them.

It's not hard to imagine which of the two responses would be more helpful to your coworker. Many of us believe expressing kindness is important and can even be life-changing for the people around us. So why wouldn't self-kindness be just as powerful? Kristin Neff, one of the leading researchers of self-compassion, compares it to being your own ally, rather than your own worst enemy.

Not surprisingly, research shows that higher levels of self-compassion are correlated with lower levels of depression and anxiety. Research even demonstrates that self-compassion can lead to experiencing higher levels of happiness, optimism, creativity, and other positive emotions.

That's why I am so committed to this work and bringing self-compassion to others. It's not just feel-good cheerleading. Self-compassion is proven to have powerful benefits and helps us show up in the world in a meaningful way.

Why We Need Self-Compassion

The hustle and bustle of modern life doesn't necessarily foster a lot of self-compassion. We're expected to be as efficient as possible and produce, produce, produce. We create all kinds of metrics to determine how much and how well we're doing in comparison to others. These expectations can quickly and easily become overwhelming and take the joy out of our work and daily lives.

When we're self-critical and hold ourselves to unrealistic standards, we're unable to honor our emotions and give ourselves the care we need, which can create fear and hopelessness. Our self-critic puts us in survival mode. We can't mess up, lest we be met with a barrage of name-calling and a feeling of despair. This kind of persistent, underlying stress wears on our mental, emotional, and physical health. The belief that our life depends on getting everything right can hold us in a never-ending cycle of pain and disappointment. It can paralyze us, keeping us from reaching for the things we want most. Self-critical thoughts lead to overwhelming emotions, which lead us to act and behave in ways that go against our values. And then the self-critic starts up again, calling us a "loser" for our actions, and the pattern repeats. If we don't acknowledge that these self-critical thoughts are harmful and unnecessary, we could spend a lifetime in this cycle.

We may think we need self-criticism for motivation. On the surface, being harsh with ourselves seems to push us to be better. But research does not support this belief. Research actually shows that self-compassion is much more intrinsically motivating. A harsh inner critic can make the fear of failure so frightening that we don't even attempt to do the thing we're afraid of, but when we practice self-compassion, we're motivated by our care and passion, our values, and those we care about.

Brené Brown's research on shame helps shed some light here. According to Brown's definition, shame is "the deep belief that we are unworthy of love and belonging," and it "is never known to lead to positive change." Shame says that you did something wrong; therefore, there's something wrong with you.

With self-compassion, you can still identify that you did something that you regret or that does not align with your values. You can admit to yourself, "Yes, I did something wrong, something outside of my values, something that doesn't align with who I am. But this doesn't make me a bad person. It's just a reminder that I need to make some changes."

Being able to recognize that your mistake does not define your worth is linked to positive change. If you believe you are more than the sum of your mistakes, there is more room for hope and motivation to change your actions to better align with who you are and how you want to show up in the world.

Self-compassion can also lead to a more meaningful life. Those who can be present with both positive and difficult experiences can access a fuller experience, which can lead to a deeper sense of fulfillment and connection with others. Research shows that highly self-compassionate folks tend to experience higher levels of happiness, optimism, creativity, and other positive emotions. If you can be more present and understanding in your pain and suffering, you can also be more present in your joy and experience your emotions on a deeper level.

Self-compassion doesn't mean a lack of accountability. Quite the opposite, actually. Self-compassion allows you to clearly identify who you are and what you value most, and it reminds you that living according to those values and intrinsic principles is possible. Self-compassion allows us to make decisions based on our personal values rather than on the fear of what others or our self-critic will say.

This approach can open up a world of possibilities. Imagine if you walked through your day meeting your struggles with kindness, believing you're worthy of compassion. Imagine the opening that could happen within your heart, your relationships, your family, and at work. Our inner critic keeps us hidden and prevents us from taking risks and connecting with others. Self-compassion allows us to identify and ask for what we need, an incredibly courageous and powerful act.

The most powerful gift of self-compassion is the internal healing it can bring. Pain, hurt, and trauma can become internalized in difficult ways. Although pain is something we all experience and aren't always responsible for, being our own worst critic only adds more pain and fear. Self-compassion is a powerful way to heal our relationship with ourselves by giving ourselves the very validation and support we most crave.

The Elements of Self-Compassion

Self-compassion is the practice of being our own ally in times of struggle and pain, which can lead to a more wholehearted and values-driven life. There are several important elements within this practice, including mindfulness, self-acceptance, grounding values, and loving-kindness.

Mindfulness: In short, mindfulness simply means paying attention. It requires you to let go of what you believe you should be thinking, feeling, or doing and just observe what is actually happening. In the acceptance and commitment therapy (ACT) model, this concept is called the observing self, the part of you that can step back from the experience of your thought or emotion and observe what's happening. It's the part of you that can identify your own judgmental thoughts. Mindfulness allows you to be present with your experience in the moment. It can help you identify your feelings, needs, and physical sensations, allowing you to take actions that are in keeping with your values and goals.

Self-acceptance: The thing I love most about self-compassion is that it doesn't require that you think you're this really awesome, amazing, wonderful person. It's not like self-esteem, which does ask that you believe you're great (maybe even special) and can be linked to comparison with others. All self-compassion asks is that you believe compassion is more helpful for humans than cruelty. If you believe kindness is good for humans, you can extend that kindness to yourself rather than beat yourself up for your flawed, or common, humanity. (Common humanity is the concept that all humans experience suffering and a range of emotions and self-doubt.) Self-compassion reminds you that you're not alone and that these experiences of suffering aren't all your fault.

Grounding in your values: What's most important to you? When you look back on your life, what do you want to be clear about you and what you stood for? Identifying your values can help guide your decisions and actions and help you understand what matters most to you. Day to day, it's easy to get caught up in things that aren't the most important to us. Those days can turn into a lifetime of putting out fires or meeting others' requests and expectations rather than prioritizing our deepest values.

For instance, you may value both your personal life and your career. One of your core values may be dependability, but that doesn't mean that you have to say "yes" to every personal and work request that comes your way. When you have a clear understanding of what dependability means to you, you might see that it actually requires saying "no" and setting boundaries so that you can follow through on your commitments in all areas of your life. This allows you a broader, fuller picture of your life, enabling you to make decisions based on a wider understanding of yourself rather than on what others think you should do.

Brené Brown and her colleagues created a list of some of the most common values based on her years of research on what allows people to live "wholehearted lives." These values include gratitude, honesty, dedication, love, family, empathy, sustainability, integrity, hard work, and independence, just to name a few.

Core values are your foundation. If you are clear on your core values, you can choose to live in ways that align with those values. And when you've lost your way or majorly screwed up, rather than turning to self-criticism and perfectionism to decide whether you're enough, you can use compassion to understand where you are out of alignment with your values and your truest self, and how to get back to it. Values can guide and center you to support yourself in practical, powerful ways.

Loving-kindness: *Merriam-Webster* defines this as "tender and benevolent affection." When you apply it to yourself, loving-kindness is simply self-kindness. Being kind to yourself is no more indulgent or silly than treating a child or partner or loved one with affection. Remember that the way you treat yourself is just as important to your relationships as the way you treat others. Loving-kindness is the practice of supporting ourselves in the midst of suffering, just as we would support anyone else we love.

How to Use This Book

You might be thinking, "This all sounds great. But how do I actually do it?" The thought of trying to go from a lifetime of self-criticism and perfectionism to a more self-compassionate way of being can be overwhelming at first. The good news is anyone can develop self-compassion. Just like building muscle or learning to cook, most of us have the capacity to learn and develop a new skill. It's important to view self-compassion as a practice that you are learning a little each day rather than another avenue for perfectionism. Even as a psychotherapist who talks about self-compassion daily with dozens of people, it is still and always will be a practice for me. I've come a long way since I first learned about self-compassion, but daily exercises, reminders, and repetition are still vital for me as my self-compassion practice continues to expand.

In this book, you'll learn practical strategies that you can easily include in your daily life. We'll focus on your thoughts, emotions, and actions to develop an effective, integrated practice that will begin to feel more natural over time. The strategies that you find most helpful will serve as anchors for you as you continue to build your skills. When you notice your inner critic revving up, you'll be able to use several tools to refocus and ground yourself in compassion and your core values.

As you read, you'll find an array of exercises such as writing and drawing prompts, meditations, gentle movements, breathing techniques, thought exercises, and more. Not every exercise will resonate with you. That's okay. It's helpful to experiment with different strategies to find what works best for you. If trying every exercise feels overwhelming at first, perhaps choose those that you are most drawn to as well as one or two that cause some resistance. Be exceptionally kind to yourself and mindful if you feel resistance. This can often indicate that the exercise is hitting on something important and tender for you, so be mindful not to push yourself too quickly.

While most of the exercises can stand alone, they are designed to build on each other, increasing your insight and skills naturally through each section.

I try to keep exercises and strategies as simple as possible because the actual inner work self-compassion elicits is anything but simple. Your self-criticism has been trying to protect you for so long. Letting go of it and allowing yourself to see things in a new way can feel painful, difficult, and/or slow going at first.

Although the concepts and strategies in this book can be incredibly helpful to your personal growth, it is important to remember that this book does not contain medical advice and is not meant to provide mental health therapy or take the place of psychotherapy or medical treatment. If you find this work to be exceptionally painful, it may be wise to consider seeking a professional who can help.

Getting Started

The exercises in this book can be easily implemented into your daily routine. Some may take as little as five minutes to complete, or you may find that with new exercises and new ways of thinking you need more time to digest and reflect on what they mean for you personally. The important thing to remember is that there's no one right way to do it.

Self-compassion is most powerful when it is integrated into a daily routine, but there's no such thing as a perfect practice. Building up to a daily self-compassion habit will give you the most opportunities to understand how to incorporate this vital skill into your life. It will allow self-kindness to become part of your routine and remind your brain that it can use these tools during times of struggle. But give yourself time to implement these exercises at your own pace. Aiming for a daily practice might mean you practice three to five days per week—that's great! Eventually, you'll find your own natural rhythm as the self-compassion tools become more accessible to you.

If you miss a day here and there, remind yourself that as a flawed human being learning something new, it's totally okay. When you notice pain or resistance come up, go back to the beginning. Start with mindfulness and ask yourself what you need. Note one or two of the exercises that really stick with you, and go back to those when you're struggling the most. Remember, try to avoid being critical of yourself for not being compassionate enough.

You've already shown so much courage in picking up this book and getting to this point. It would be easy to throw it aside and keep doing what's comfortable. But you are committed to yourself and to a path of wholehearted living. The willingness to take the steps is all you need. Remember, courage does not mean you're not afraid. Courage is being afraid but doing it anyway!

Self-Compassion Scale

Before beginning the exercises, complete the following scale (created by Kristine Neff, Ph.D.) to get a general idea of your current self-compassion levels. After you've finished this workbook, revisiting the scale will allow you to measure your growing self-compassion. Growth can happen gradually over time, which makes it hard for us to fully grasp the progress we make day to day. With self-criticism, growth can be especially hard to see. Consider your scores here as helpful information, and be careful not to use them as more fodder for self-criticism.

If you find yourself bummed by your scores, remember, that's exactly why you picked up this book. If your scores are better than you expected, that's wonderful! Know that this book will support and strengthen your practice with tangible tools for your everyday life.

HOW I TYPICALLY ACT TOWARD MYSELF IN DIFFICULT TIMES

Please read each statement carefully before answering. To the left of each item, indicate how often you behave in the stated manner, using the following scale:

Almost Never   **Almost Always**
         1   2   3   4   5

_____ When I fail at something important to me, I become consumed by feelings of inadequacy.

_____ I try to be understanding and patient with aspects of my personality that I don't like.

_____ When something painful happens, I try to take a balanced view of the situation.

_____ When I'm feeling down, I tend to feel most other people are probably happier than I am.

_____ I try to see my failings as part of the human condition.

_____ When I'm going through a very hard time, I give myself the caring and tenderness I need.

_____ When something upsets me, I try to keep my emotions in balance.

_____ When I fail at something that's important to me, I tend to feel alone in my failure.

_____ When I'm feeling down, I tend to obsess and fixate on everything that's wrong.

_____ When I feel inadequate in some way, I try to remind myself that feelings of inadequacy are shared by most people.

_____ I'm disapproving and judgmental about my own flaws and inadequacies.

_____ I'm intolerant and impatient with aspects of my personality I don't like.

Scoring your test:

Total (sum of all 12 items) _____

Average score (Total divided by 12) _____

According to Kristin Neff's research, an average self-compassion score is close to 3.0. Use the following as a general guide:

Higher levels of self-compassion: scores of 3.5 to 5.0

Average/moderate levels of self-compassion: scores of 2.5 to 3.5

Lower levels of self-compassion: scores of 1 to 2.5

PART TWO

Self-Compassion and Thoughts

If self-compassion is talking to yourself like you'd talk to a loved one, then you'll first need to address your self-critical thoughts to begin to shift your inner talk. In this section, you'll learn strategies for observing and adjusting your thoughts to be more helpful, adaptive, and self-compassionate.

Thoughts vs. Reality

" . . . our main interest in a thought is not whether it's true or false, but whether it's helpful; that is, if we pay attention to this thought, will it help us create the life we want?"

—Russ Harris, *The Happiness Trap:*
How to Stop Struggling and Start Living

The average human has thousands of thoughts per day. For most of us, thoughts feel automatic and often uncontrollable. We use these automatic thoughts to determine what's true about the world. However, we also know that two people can experience the same event and come away with very different stories. Those of us who struggle with a deep inner critic often have a hard time separating ourselves from our own critical thoughts.

For instance, Keisha feels guilty for forgetting to send a friend's birthday gift and has the self-critical thought, "I'm not a very good friend." Although Keisha's friend is understanding and reassures Keisha over and over about all the ways she has been a good friend, Keisha can't shake her critical thoughts and feelings. Keisha's critical inner voice says, "She's just saying that to be nice, but I really screwed up, and there's nothing I can do to make it better."

Without understanding how to mindfully observe her thinking to better understand and process it, Keisha may obsess about this mistake for days, weeks, or even months.

Keisha has fused with her thoughts. Imagine Keisha's thoughts as a metal plate, welded together with her feelings and actions. There's no room to consider that she's anything but a terrible friend, so Keisha's behavior becomes controlled by her impulsive thinking. She struggles to even accept the perspective of a trusted friend. She may start to avoid her friend because she feels so bad about her mistake. She may start to feel like she's a bad friend to her other friends as well and may begin to feel depressed or anxious.

We can be fused to all kinds of thoughts, but this attachment to self-critical thoughts can be especially harmful. These thoughts are often cognitive distortions, patterns of thinking that are inaccurate, unhelpful, or even hurtful to our own well-being and functioning.

Some of the cognitive distortions Keisha exhibits in this example are based on emotional reasoning ("I feel guilty; therefore, I must have done something wrong"), all-or-nothing or perfectionist thinking ("I'm either always a good friend or I'm the worst"), or disqualifying the positive ("My friend's opinion doesn't matter because she's just being nice"). Keisha also experiences rumination—repetitive thinking over and over about the mistake—specifically, the negative parts of the situation and how it's all her fault.

These thinking patterns have turned Keisha's moment of forgetfulness into a painful, days-long spiral of self-criticism. Meanwhile, her friend is happily enjoying her birthday and looking forward to gifts continuing to come in later. Keisha's fusion to her self-critical thinking keeps her from being able to be fully present and engaged in celebrating her friend.

Now, let's say Keisha tries different strategies when this negative thinking first comes up. Keisha realizes her birthday gift will be late, and the same thoughts of being a bad friend start to float through her brain. She reminds herself that she does not have to automatically fuse with these thoughts but that she can pause and examine the thought for what it is (just a thought). Then, she can identify whether this thought is helpful or not and begin to better understand what would be helpful. Perhaps Keisha takes a few deep breaths and says to herself, "It's hard when I don't meet my own expectations of what a friend should be. But all I can do is my best. Mistakes happen. I will get the gift as soon as I can, but what's most important is being able to celebrate with my friend!"

Take a moment to notice the difference between these types of thinking patterns, and imagine which one might feel more helpful in the moment if you were in Keisha's shoes. The following exercises will help you learn to recognize your critical thoughts for what they are (just thoughts), learn how to pay more attention to your thoughts, and practice more helpful and self-compassionate thinking that will support you in creating the life you want.

Taking Note of Your Inner Critic

It often feels easier to try to ignore our inner critic. We think we're better off pushing it to the side, never acknowledging it or sitting with it long enough to really hear what it's saying. It's obviously a bit scary to face our inner critic. But if we don't really understand it and how it sounds, it's hard for us to address our critical thinking in a helpful way. We end up sweeping these thoughts under the rug. However, rather than disappear, the things we sweep under the rug build and build, often tripping us up and having more power over us than they would have if we had addressed them head-on.

As you're reading this book, you've likely started identifying your inner critic and some of its common messages. Take a moment to think about a recent time when you found yourself in a difficult moment or upset about a mistake.

Set the stage. What happened? What led up to this difficult moment?

What thoughts came up? Did you notice any thoughts that really hooked you, that kept coming up again and again?

Examples: Not being able to stop thinking about that one thing you said that you feel bad about or harping on a mistake you made.

What did you believe about yourself in that moment? What self-critical messages came up?

Examples: I can't believe I made that mistake. I'm a total failure. I knew I shouldn't have even tried that. Of course, I'd fail.

What was the first thing you wanted to do?

Examples: Curling up in a ball, running away, or screaming. Can you notice if these impulses were connected to any of the self-critical thoughts you wrote about in the previous question?

Are there any thoughts that you identified that, looking back, don't appear to be facts or that you're willing to consider might not be totally true?

Examples: Making a mistake doesn't mean that I, as a person, am a total failure. Just because something I said led to conflict doesn't mean my feeling or opinion shouldn't be shared.

TIP: If it's hard for you to identify these thoughts right now, that's okay. They can be so automatic that it's hard to really see them. Your tactics to avoid facing critical thoughts may also be automatic, so getting around those to really see what's happening takes time and practice as well. Do the best you can here, and then keep moving through the exercises.

Fusing with the Critic

To illustrate how seeing your self-critical thoughts as facts and allowing them to take hold can affect you, try the following exercise.

On a piece of paper, write down some common thoughts you identified from your inner critic in the previous exercise. Now, hold the paper right in front of your face, just touching your nose.

After sitting like this for a few moments, briefly write about your experience. How does the world around you look with the paper blocking your view? Can you easily interact and connect with others in this position? Can you even read the thoughts you wrote down to understand what's actually blocking your view?

....

....

....

....

Now, experiment with slowly moving the paper farther away from your face. Perhaps move it just far enough that you can read the thoughts you wrote down.

Take note of your view now. How does the world around you look now that you've moved the paper slightly? Do you have a better sense of the environment around you? Do you have more ability to interact and connect with others? Do you have more awareness of what's blocking your view now and what to do about it?

....

....

....

You can think of this as the point where you are now in this book. You are learning to pull the paper away and read those self-critical thoughts. You're gaining knowledge and awareness of which thoughts are taking hold of you, but it's still difficult to see around them and sometimes overwhelming to not know what to do next.

Continue to experiment with moving the paper farther away, as far as your arm will reach straight in front of you. Then, begin to move the paper down or to the side. Again, moving slowly, take note of what you can and can't see.

How differently can you interact with the world around you now that your critical thoughts are no longer blocking your view?

JUAN'S STORY

Juan's having a tough day. Work has been busy, and he got some negative feedback on his performance from his boss recently. Money is tight, which makes Juan even more anxious about his job. He feels like the only way to keep his metaphorical ship afloat is to work himself to the bone. All day at work and on his way home, his inner critic says, "You aren't good enough or doing enough. You can't rest. No one will ever be satisfied with everything you do."

When Juan arrives home, his partner is cooking dinner, the dogs are barking, and there's a pile of dishes in the sink. His partner says, "Hey, so glad you're home. Can you take the dogs out while I finish cooking?"

Despite dog walking being a typical part of his routine, Juan hits his breaking point, "You expect me to do everything! I work all day to keep us afloat, but it's still not enough." He huffs, "I can never rest, and it's never good enough for you!"

Juan's self-critical thinking leads him to interpret a simple interaction with his partner as validation of his own painful thoughts and fears. His explosion is due to his inner critic, but it's projected onto his partner.

This happens often in relationships. We all have inner critics and triggers that we project on those closest to us, which can lead to disconnection if we aren't mindful of what's really happening.

If we can develop more awareness and understanding of this thinking, we can begin to learn from these interactions and work through them with our loved ones in a way that develops deeper connection and understanding of one another and ourselves.

Thoughts as Clouds

Learning to hold self-critical thoughts more loosely begins with practicing simple mindful awareness. Use this meditative exercise to practice what it's like to observe your thoughts without judging them or immediately assuming they're true.

1. Find a quiet, comfortable place where you won't be disturbed for at least a few minutes. If it helps, set a timer to encourage yourself to practice without watching the clock. If you've never practiced meditation before, start small, setting the timer for one to five minutes.

2. Close your eyes gently if it feels comfortable, and ground yourself by taking a few slow, deep breaths.

3. Picture a bright blue sky full of puffy, white clouds. Take a few moments to breathe into that image.

4. When you're ready, take each thought that comes up and place it on a cloud. Do this with every thought, no matter how wonderful or difficult the thought seems.

5. When difficult thoughts or feelings come up, simply name or observe them. "Here's a feeling of discomfort," or "I'm having the thought that this exercise is silly." Rather than considering the thoughts as good or bad, try thinking of them as helpful or unhelpful.

6. Continue observing your thoughts and allowing them to float by in their own way and in their own time. There might be thoughts that seem to stick around longer than others. There's no need to force thoughts to move at a certain speed or to go away. Your goal is simply to observe your thoughts as they happen in the present moment.

7. If your mind wanders, take note of it, without judgment, and then come back to the blue sky, starting again with the clouds.

TIP: Don't worry if you struggle with visualization. Being mindful during a creative activity may allow you to be less judgmental and more able to pay attention to the present moment. Try writing your thoughts down, coloring, or working on a puzzle while you practice observing your thoughts without judgment.

Facts vs. Judgments

This simple exercise can help us recognize that the thoughts we tend to view as facts are actually subjective judgments or opinions. This can be another helpful strategy in defusing yourself from your thoughts. Even if it is your thought, it's still just an opinion. Call it what it is!

Here are some examples of facts versus judgments:

FACTS	JUDGMENTS
I slept through my alarm this morning.	I'm lazy and worthless.
I yelled at my kid today.	I'm a big jerk.
I got a failing grade.	I'll never amount to anything.

Write out some thoughts about yourself as they come up. Feel free to use thoughts you wrote down from any previous exercises, or just use thoughts off the top of your head.

Go back and circle any thoughts that are judgments, not facts. (It may be all of them—that's okay.)

Self-critical judgments often start with some actual event or fact, as you can see from the example list at the beginning of this exercise. For each judgment you circled, do your best to restate it as a fact.

FACTS	JUDGMENTS

BONUS: Using one or more of the fact statements you identified, write a response that's more self-compassionate than your initial judgment. Think about how a friend might rephrase that judgmental thought or how you might rephrase it if a friend told you they had that critical thought.

FACTS	SELF-COMPASSIONATE RESPONSE
I slept through my alarm today.	I must have been really exhausted.
I yelled at my kid today.	It's painful when I lose my temper with them.

Not *That* Special

Sometimes our inner critic leads us to believe that we are somehow especially bad or deserving of the pain and suffering we experience. But being a human being is hard. We all know what it's like to struggle. There's likely someone in the world who has had an experience or feeling similar to yours—maybe not exactly the same but similar enough to be able to empathize with you and remind you that you're not alone. As I mentioned before, self-compassion isn't about believing you're better or more special than anyone else (as with self-esteem), and it starts with understanding that struggle is a universal human experience.

Think about an instance when a close friend, loved one, or even a character in your favorite story has struggled with something and appeared to feel bad about themselves.

_____

_____

_____

How might you respond in a kind or helpful way to the person in that situation? What would you say and how would you treat them?

_____

_____

_____

_____

How have you responded to yourself when you have experienced a similar struggle? Take note of how you tend to talk to yourself, your tone of voice, and how you treat yourself in these moments.

Is there a difference between how you treat yourself and someone else in the same situation? Why do you think that is? In other words, what makes you so special that you deserve such different treatment?

What would change if you could respond to yourself more like you would to a dear friend?

Below are some statements that help remind us of our common humanity, of how we are connected with others and not isolated in our struggles. Circle the ones that feel most helpful now or write your own.

"There are probably thousands of people who have felt the way I do."

"I'm not alone."

"It must be hard to live with this inner critic every day."

"Struggle is a normal part of life."

AFFIRMATION

This is tough work you're doing right now! Identifying, exploring, and digging through the depths of our self-critic is no joke. You might have noticed pain, overwhelm, resistance, avoidance, or even anger come up with some of these exercises. Resistance to pain or uncertainty is a completely normal human reaction.

If you notice these thoughts or emotions come up, first of all, it's okay to pause. Take a deep breath. Take your time. This process doesn't need to be rushed. Give yourself permission to do this work at your own pace.

I often joke that some of my favorite self-compassion and therapeutic books, while written in very accessible language, can take me a very long time to read. It feels like every chapter (or even every page) stirs up so much for me to process. I have to take it one step at a time.

So please, remember, it's okay to take it slowly. When you notice resistance or pain come up, go back to the tools you've worked on so far. Be mindful. Take a breath. Observe without judgment. Say, "Here's a feeling of resistance."

This is a lifelong practice that will become easier over time. It's okay if it's not all coming naturally right away!

Should-ing on Yourself

Your inner critic may show up as a should-er. Maybe it doesn't say rude things like "You're an idiot." Instead, it may hold you to impossibly high standards. "Should" statements often function like rigid rules that can be unhelpful and lead to painful self-criticism and perfectionism. Use the following questions to better understand your self-critical should statements and to develop more helpful thinking.

Examples of should statements: "To be a good parent I should show up to every single little league game," or "I should exercise six days a week in order to be healthy."

1. Should-ing on Yourself: Think about a time when you felt bad about yourself, and write down what you thought you should have done instead.

....

....

....

....

....

2. Defining the "Should":

    What "rule" did you break? Why did you feel so bad about it?

....

....

....

Where do you think this rule came from? What about it feels important to you?

_____

_____

_____

_____

3. Nonjudgmental Evaluation:

How does this "should" help you?

_____

_____

_____

How is this "should" unhelpful or even hurtful to you?

_____

_____

_____

4. What's Next? Sometimes, a "should" is so extreme or hurtful, we're ready to let it go of it altogether. Other times, we're not ready to do that yet, perhaps because we've used it as a critical guide for so long. Taking everything into consideration so far, where are you with your should statement(s)?

....

....

....

....

5. The Value: Rather than letting go of a "should" completely, it may be most helpful to modify it to be a more realistic and compassionate reflection of your values.

Here are some examples of value statements modified from the examples of should statements on page 29: "I value being involved and engaged in my child's life (even if I can't show up to every game)," or "I value my health by setting realistic expectations for my exercise routine."

Think about the values behind your "should," and rewrite your should statements in a way that more accurately depicts what's important to you.

....

....

....

....

TIP: Some people worry that letting go of this kind of thinking will lead to a loss of accountability. But that's not the case. A helpful, flexible rule in the form of a grounding value can help us gain clarity about our choices and can motivate us to be our best selves. We'll continue to explore values throughout the book.

The Magic Wand

When we're stuck in a spiral of self-criticism, distortions, and should statements, it can be hard to see a way out. Sometimes, experimenting with a creative or fun idea can help get us unstuck. By giving yourself permission to experiment with the idea that you can reach your ultimate self-compassion goal, you open up new ways of thinking, which may allow you to recognize what you actually can do right now to become more self-compassionate.

1. Imagine that you have a magic wand that really works. I'm serious. Grab your wand, and wave it around a bit. Get into it!

2. Your wand gives you the power to stop your self-critical thoughts from hooking you. You're able to call up self-compassion any time you want.

3. Imagine waking up tomorrow with this new reality. What's different? What are your thoughts like? How does this begin to change how you think, function, feel, and act?

4. Draw what this new reality looks and feels like. Creativity can help us more fully process abstract concepts. Don't overthink it. This is a fun exercise; it doesn't need to be a masterpiece.

5. Is there anything about this magical new reality that seems believable for you? What's one thing you could change tomorrow that may allow you to get closer to that reality?

Examples: If your magic wand helps you have more self-compassionate thinking, start each day by reading a self-compassionate quote or repeating a mantra. Or, if your magic wand takes away your self-punishing behavior of denying yourself needed self-care, try doing something you usually deny yourself, like reading for a half hour, calling a friend just to hear their voice, or taking a nap.

TIP: If you're getting stuck because this feels silly, unbelievable, or pointless, remember— this is a simple experiment. Imagine it as a movie plot or that you're telling a child a story. You can say to yourself, "I don't really believe this, but I'll let myself dive into this story for a moment just to see what it's like."

Thoughts of Loving-Kindness

Learning to practice mindful loving-kindness with our thoughts can help us practice more self-compassionate thinking and avoid the cycle of being critical of our own self-criticism. This exercise may feel strange at first, but remember that the more you practice, the more natural and helpful these skills will become.

1. Find a quiet space for yourself, even if it's just a few minutes in the car before you leave for work. Close your eyes, and take several deep breaths.

2. Now imagine a person or being who loves you deeply, sitting right next to you. This could be a real person from any time in your life, a spiritual guide or being, or even an older, wiser version of yourself.

3. Allow yourself to feel their love, care, warmth, and well-wishes for you.

4. Imagine that this being knows about these difficult thoughts you're having. Begin to imagine what they'd say and how they would comfort you. Let yourself sink into their kindness, their love, their light.

5. Perhaps you can imagine them repeating the following:

    May you hold your thoughts loosely.
    May you allow them to float by with ease.
    May you be filled with thoughts of loving-kindness.
    May you accept yourself as you are.

6. Take a few more mindful breaths and notice what it's like to allow yourself and your thoughts to be surrounded by loving-kindness. Repeat these phrases (or others of your own) to yourself:

    May I hold my thoughts loosely.
    May I allow them to float by with ease.
    May I be filled with thoughts of loving-kindness.
    May I accept myself just as I am.

SARA'S STORY

Sara has a fear of flying. Before her flight, she begins to feel anxious, her heart races, and her palms become sweaty. The danger feels real, and Sara begins to worry about what others might think when they notice her anxiety.

"I'm so ridiculous," she thinks. "Why am I always so weak and scared? Why can't I just act like an adult and get over it?"

Unfortunately, this line of thinking doesn't take her anxious feelings away, and now she feels more anxious and shameful about her own anxiety. What a painful cycle!

Sara texts her cousin, Ross, who also experiences anxiety. Thankfully, he's able to respond before Sara boards her flight. "Sara, I'm so sorry you're feeling that way. Flying can be scary. Tons of people (including me) have anxiety about flying. Remember to take deep breaths and be kind to yourself."

Ross's compassion allows Sara to acknowledge that her anxiety is a very human response to a fairly new human experience (historically speaking). Flying in an airplane, while statistically very safe, still has risks, as do most things humans do. Anxiety is a natural part of how our minds and bodies protect ourselves.

In Sara's case, trying to avoid, deny, or criticize her own difficult emotions was not helpful. Criticizing our struggles in this way is likely to trigger even more anxiety, frustration, and shame. It can also cut us off from the mindful awareness that helps us recognize what thoughts and practices may actually be helpful to us (in Sara's case, deep breaths and more self-compassionate thinking).

Although helpful reminders from friends and loved ones are always welcome, imagine how much easier it would be if Sara could practice more self-compassion with her anxiety when the self-criticism first appears.

Your Own Self-Compassion Mantra

A mantra is a statement or phrase you repeat to remind yourself of your personal beliefs and values. Self-compassion mantras can be great tools to remind you of the helpful thoughts and beliefs you're working to cultivate.

1. Use the Elements of Self-Compassion (page 5) along with what you've learned in the previous exercises to begin to build your own personal mantra. Each exercise from this section links to one or more of the elements, so feel free to refer to them to help you create phrases that are most helpful to you.

Mindfulness (Taking Note of Your Inner Critic, Fusing with the Critic, and Thoughts as Clouds exercises)

Examples: Oh, this is really hard for me. Take a breath.

....

....

....

Self-acceptance (Facts vs. Judgments and Not *That* Special exercises)

Examples: It's normal to feel this way. I'm not alone in this.

....

....

....

Grounding in your values (Should-ing on Yourself and The Magic Wand exercises)

Examples: I don't have to be perfect. Love is more powerful than fear.

....

....

....

Loving-kindness (The Magic Wand and Thoughts of Loving-Kindness exercises)

Examples: May I be compassionate. May I be patient with myself.

....

....

....

2. Now, put it all together. You can combine all four elements or keep it shorter—whatever feels most helpful for you.

Example: Take a breath. It's normal to struggle. In this moment, may I accept myself as I am.

....

....

....

....

....

....

3. If you can, write your mantra on a card or sticky note, and place it where you will see it regularly. Say it to yourself at least once daily. The more you practice your mantra in neutral times, the more naturally you will be able to remember it when your inner critic pipes up.

TIP: Sometimes, your mantra may help you shift to self-compassionate thinking immediately. Other times, you may need to repeat it over and over (and over!) again. That's okay. Keep repeating it until you can actually hear and follow the words. The mantra will serve as a distraction from escalating critical thoughts until your mind and body have fully integrated the tools in this book.

Notice the Difference: Self-Critical Response vs. Self-Compassionate Response

Ginger is a hardworking attorney and new mom in her late 30s. Her job is very important to her, and she's worked tirelessly to get to this point in her career. She loves being a mom and wants to spend as much time with her baby as she can. However, Ginger is becoming more and more exhausted trying to keep up with work and family life at the very high standards she has set for herself. She's becoming more irritable with her partner and finds herself feeling resentful about all the responsibilities she has taken on in the past year.

Self-Critical Response

Think about how Ginger's inner critic might respond to her exhaustion and irritability. Write that response here.

Example: You just can't hack it. You'll never be able to do enough.

....

....

....

Self-Compassionate Response

Now write a self-compassionate response to Ginger's experience.

Example: You're juggling so much right now and still adjusting to being a parent—none of this is easy. Remember it's okay to accept that you may not be able to do everything perfectly.

....

....

....

Mental Benefits of Self-Compassion

When you picked up this workbook, I'm sure you already had some ideas about how self-compassion might be helpful. But facing your inner critic and really diving in can bring up resistance and fear. That's why it's important to remember the point of this difficult work, to remember your why for developing a self-compassion practice.

Research shows that increased self-compassion can protect against anxiety and depression. Even if you still have a lot of self-critical thinking, the practice of self-compassion can lead to less rumination, especially about your own weaknesses and flaws. When our fusion to negative thoughts decreases, we can enjoy less anxious thinking and an overall improved mood. Greater levels of self-compassion can also lead to increased resiliency after difficult experiences, healthier coping skills, and increased intrinsic motivation (motivation that comes from our own inner values rather than external rewards).

As you've seen in many of the examples in this book, the increased self-awareness that comes from practicing self-compassion changes the way we interact and think about our relationships as well. When you can see your self-critic for what it is, you're less likely to project those beliefs onto the people who care about you, and you're more likely to reach out for support when you most need it.

Hopefully, you're already beginning to see some of these benefits as you practice these exercises. However, it's possible that you feel more resistant to self-compassion than you did when you began. Or maybe you see the benefits, but your inner perfectionist is frustrated by your learning curve. Whatever is coming up is okay! This is a perfect time to practice self-compassion, take a breath, observe your thoughts nonjudgmentally, and treat yourself with kindness.

PART THREE

Self-Compassion and Emotions

Emotions are sticky things. We often try to ignore or control them, which is why the emotions keep coming up. In this section, you'll learn how to manage your emotions with self-compassion rather than try to control or eliminate them (because those methods just don't work).

Separating Feelings from Facts

When your brain identifies something threatening or dangerous, it jump-starts a full-body response, activating your nervous system and pumping adrenaline and cortisol (also known as the stress hormone) throughout your body. Your heart races, your muscles tense, and you might sweat or begin to develop fast, shallow breathing. This is known as the survival or fight-or-flight response. It is an important mechanism when you're in a truly dangerous situation (like a truck barreling down the road at you) and you don't have the luxury to calmly think through what to do. However, this response can lead us to feel that our emotions themselves are dangerous.

We tend to seek certainty as a form of safety, and our emotions rarely feel clear and certain. As a result, we may internalize some feelings as truth about ourselves or the environment around us. For instance, when we feel weak or ashamed, we may see this as evidence that we are actually unworthy. Seeing our emotions as facts can also lead us into a cycle of self-criticism. For example, if feeling anger leads you to believe that you're a bad, angry person, then you may criticize yourself to address this "fact." We can be so fused with our thoughts and emotions that we can't see things through any other lens.

While our emotions may not always represent facts, they can provide useful information about ourselves, what we're experiencing, and what might be helpful to us. When we try to avoid, numb, or criticize our own emotions, we end up abandoning and invalidating whole parts of ourselves. Those emotions that we push to the side don't actually go away. They stay in the background, piling up, until something triggers them and causes them to overflow. This may result in you lashing out or having a general sense of frustration, restlessness, or anxiety that you can never quite pinpoint. The more you ignore or invalidate your emotions, the more they control you.

Accepting our emotions opens up space for us to understand them. It allows us to access a deeper part of ourselves and to build a level of awareness that's not possible when we're constantly fusing with or judging our feelings. Recognizing emotion enables us to show ourselves compassion around what's affecting us.

Emotional exposure can feel dangerous to our brain and body, which means that emotions themselves can become threatening. To tolerate this discomfort, we have to find a way to create safety while we're experiencing vulnerable emotions. This is where self-compassion comes in. When your self-critic is bearing down on every negative emotion you have, not only is the emotion itself scary, but you also live in fear of the wrath of your inner critic. So, when you feel deep sadness or hurt, you may fear that you're emotionally weak or incapable. Or when you feel anxious, you may feel fearful that you're being irrational and overreacting.

Self-compassion allows us to show up for ourselves with support in these difficult moments. In a moment of deep sadness or grief, self-compassion says, "This is a difficult situation. It's normal to feel down and unmotivated right now." When you experience anxiety, self-compassion might offer, "This is really scary for you. Everyone has worries. What would be helpful right now?"

The goal of self-compassion is not to eliminate all difficult emotional experiences but to allow them to exist without resisting or suppressing them. We start by accepting emotions as a normal human experience. Then, rather than act as our own enemy in these moments by criticizing ourselves for having emotions, we can show up as an ally, a supportive friend, in the midst of struggle.

In the following exercises, you'll learn steps to accept and identify your emotions, replace self-criticism with emotional curiosity, and use helpful strategies to create a feeling of safety in your mind and body. These steps are part of your continued journey to create a personal self-compassion practice that can lead to powerful change in your day-to-day life.

Permission to Feel

Our inner critic often tells us what we should or shouldn't do, and it doesn't allow much room for uncertainty, imperfection, or messy emotions. If we can start by giving ourselves permission for our very human emotions and struggles–rather than trying to avoid or criticize ourselves for them–we'll be able to process our emotions, practice mindful awareness, and better understand what we need.

Think about what it might take to give yourself permission to fully feel your emotions. Use the prompts below to identify what permission would be most helpful for you. I've included examples to help get you started.

What holds you back? Where do you get stuck? What are you afraid might happen if you allowed yourself to feel the full range of your emotions? Write about this in the lines below.

....

....

....

....

When I'm overcome with emotion, I'm afraid . . .

Examples: I'll lose control, others will judge me, it will be too much for anyone to handle

....

....

When I notice big emotions, I tend to . . .

Examples: get quiet, tell myself I'm being ridiculous, lash out at others

....

....

If I could allow myself to feel my emotions without judging them immediately,
I could . . .

Examples: identify my emotion, console myself, reach out for support

....

....

Complete the sentences below, using a feeling word that represents an emotion
that you often resist experiencing.

It's okay to feel ....

When I have this feeling, I give myself permission to ....

....

Just because I feel ...., it doesn't

necessarily mean ....

....

I give myself permission to feel ....

....

Labeling Emotions

Many people struggle with identifying how they really feel in detail. Being able to name various types of emotions allows you to better understand your own needs and show yourself compassion.

Here's a chart of complex emotion words under their more general counterparts.

HAPPY	MAD	SAD	ANXIOUS
Excited	Angry	Hurt	Fearful
Comfortable	Enraged	Remorseful	Distressed
Grateful	Agitated	Heartbroken	Nervous
Content	Resentful	Grieving	Restless
Joyous	Distracted	Bitter	Uneasy
Peaceful	Rejected	Distraught	Stressed
Thrilled	Frantic	Melancholy	Doubtful
Upbeat	Exasperated	Disillusioned	Concerned
Relieved	Shocked	Ashamed	Uncertain

Choose several emotion words that you don't typically use. Write about a time you felt that way and what might differentiate that feeling from the other emotions listed in the chart.

Emotion word: _____

Your experience with this emotion: _____

_____

_____

_____

How is this emotion different from others in the same column?

_____

_____

_____

_____

Emotion word: _____

Your experience with this emotion: _____

_____

_____

_____

How is this emotion different from others in the same column?

_____

_____

_____

Emotion word: _____

Your experience with this emotion: _____

_____

_____

_____

_____

How is this emotion different from others in the same column?

_____

_____

_____

_____

TIP: If you're struggling, feel free to look up the dictionary definitions of the words. Use one of the anecdotes from this book and identify the possible emotions the character felt or that you might have felt in a similar situation. Know that the differences between the emotions can be hard to put into words. It might be helpful to think of how the emotion feels in your body or what types of situations might trigger it.

GREG'S STORY

Greg struggles with social anxiety. He often gets very frustrated with himself for this, telling himself he's being ridiculous and that he should just get over it. While Greg and his wife are driving to a friend's wedding, Greg begins to feel overwhelmed and anxious about all the new people he'll have to meet and make small talk with. He tells himself he's just being stupid and acting like a baby. Greg's wife notices his distress and, trying to help, reassures him that everyone there will be kind and that they can spend most of their time with the people they already know. "Don't you think I know that?" Greg retorts angrily.

Rather than feel supported by his wife's reassurances, Greg experiences them as proving his own self-critic right. To his inner critic, he must be weak and ridiculous if he doesn't already know the facts his wife points out. Now Greg not only feels anxious about the wedding but also ashamed of his own emotions and worried that his wife shares his inner critic's opinion of him as stupid and childish.

Self-compassion may not take Greg's social anxiety away, but it could help Greg find a way to support himself in these difficult moments rather than add to his distress by judging his emotional reactions.

Greg's self-compassionate voice might say, "Here's a feeling of anxiety. I've experienced this before. A lot of people have a fear of big crowds and hate small talk." When he's not stuck in a cycle of self-judgment about his anxiety, it might be easier for him to remember to do breathing techniques or to see his wife's words as supportive.

Although self-compassion won't eliminate difficult emotions, you can see how it can bring powerful change to these distressing experiences.

Emotions as Information

What if there isn't a right or wrong way to feel? What would happen if you replaced criticism of your emotions with curiosity?

As a child, you may have been told not to cry or learned that certain emotions or reactions didn't seem acceptable to others. These messages can become internalized and lead us to blame or judge ourselves for our emotions, which come and go much in the same way our thoughts do.

Rather than seeing your emotions as something you must immediately control, what if you saw them simply as information? Think about your emotions as the dashboard on your car. Obviously, running low on oil or gas can be frustrating, but we'd rather know and keep our car in tune than end up on the side of the road with no idea what's wrong.

1. Choose an emotion (perhaps from the chart on page 48), and use the mindfulness skills you learned in part 2 to name the emotion. Say, "Here's a feeling of frustration." Or you might say, "Here's a feeling of deep remorse."

2. Notice what the emotion feels like—where it shows up in your body, what the experience is like. Take some deep breaths to allow yourself space to feel.

3. Remind yourself that you can allow this emotion to float by without criticizing it or pushing it away.

4. Thank this emotion for showing up and for providing you with information.

5. If you notice a feeling of discomfort or avoidance, go through this process again. Start with "Here's a feeling of discomfort." Allow yourself to breathe into it, thanking yourself and the emotion for the space to feel.

Take some time to reflect and write about your experience. What information might this emotion be giving you that you'd miss if you tried to ignore or criticize it?

Anger: A Secondary Emotion

Anger is an emotion that can be especially hard to connect with compassion. Anger is known in psychology as a secondary emotion because it often operates as a protective emotion that occurs when we're feeling especially vulnerable or out of control. It may feel too painful or scary to experience the underlying emotion (such as hurt, sadness, rejection, fear, or shame), but anger may give us a semblance of control. Anger is not a bad or wrong emotion–it can be powerful and productive–but blind anger, if we don't acknowledge what's behind it, can be hurtful. Often, we use anger to hide or protect our deepest vulnerabilities while projecting our challenging emotions onto someone or something else.

Think about the last time you got angry. Write about the situation—what happened, what was said, etc.

....

....

....

Tapping into curiosity rather than judgment, write about how that experience felt for you.

It might help to consider questions like these: What did it feel like in your body? Did you feel powerful or ashamed by your anger? What did you think about yourself during or after your experience of feeling and/or acting on your anger?

....

....

....

....

Understanding anger as a secondary emotion, a way we respond when we feel threatened, write about what threat or underlying emotion may have been behind your anger.

Examples: hurt, disappointment, fear of rejection or judgment

_____

_____

_____

_____

_____

_____

Given that anger often serves as a protective measure, what might you need in order to feel safe or accepted in the moments when anger pops up? What self-compassionate messages might you send yourself?

_____

_____

_____

_____

_____

_____

You're Allowed to Be Sad

There are countless times that someone has come to me with an issue and asked me how they can stop crying about it. I always respond that crying is a way of expressing emotion, and ignoring or pushing that emotion down isn't something I encourage anyone do. Oftentimes, half of the struggle with emotions that we view as negative or uncomfortable, like sadness or grief, is dealing with our own judgment and self-criticism about having that emotion.

Has there been a time when you've felt sad or grieved about something, and someone quickly said, "Hey, don't be sad, it's all going to be okay!" or even simply, "Stop crying!"

How do responses like these make you feel?

....

....

....

When other people try to wish your sadness away, what happens? What about when you try to avoid your own sadness or wish it away?

....

....

....

....

What feels uncomfortable about your sadness that might keep you from accepting it?

....

....

....

....

Write a letter to yourself to read when you are feeling sad. Think about what words would feel most soothing and helpful from a friend or loved one. Maybe there aren't even words. Perhaps a gentle touch or sitting with you as long as you need would help. Write what feels most comforting and validating for you in a moment of deep sadness or grief.

....

....

....

....

....

....

....

....

....

TIP: This may be an especially tough exercise. Be mindful to be kind to yourself. The soothing touch exercises coming next may be exceptionally helpful if you're finding this exercise to be emotionally intense.

AFFIRMATION

What you're working through in this section is not easy. I'm asking you to sit and breathe when you just want to run from your uncomfortable emotions. I'm asking you to say it out loud when your first impulse is to keep it zipped up, hidden from everyone who might see. I'm asking you to lean into discomfort, to sit with it. That's a tall order.

Are you willing to be uncomfortable in order to do what matters to you? When this work feels too hard, remind yourself what matters most and why you picked up this book in the first place. You want to be kinder to yourself. You want to be able to create your own safe place to land when you're struggling. You want to be able to connect to your own emotions so that you can show up with true empathy for those around you. You want to show up as your authentic self in the world, and identify what matters most so you can call it up when you are feeling resistant or tired of this difficult work. You want to tap into what you value most, into what keeps you going.

Breathe into It

Our breath is an incredible tool that we can access any time to self-soothe, slow down, become mindful, and create a feeling of calm and safety in our bodies. There are countless breathing exercises and strategies that can be helpful. We'll practice one here.

This exercise can help you slow down and sit in the discomfort of your emotions when you're feeling overwhelmed. It will be most helpful if you practice it in neutral times as well; that way, your brain and body know what to do when you're in the midst of emotional discomfort.

1. Find a quiet, safe place where you won't be disturbed for a few minutes. If it's valuable to you, set a timer for 5 to 10 minutes.

2. Close your eyes and take a few full, deep breaths.

3. As you inhale, think about the oxygen that's flooding your body. Imagine it making its way into every part and cell of your body, filling you up with life.

4. If it suits you, imagine this life you're breathing in is full of compassion and warmth for you. With each inhale, imagine this love and comfort being sent into every part and every cell of your body.

5. Each time you breathe out, imagine releasing any tension, self-criticism, or resistance. Try not to push your breath out too quickly. Let it flow out with your exhale slowly and naturally.

6. Continue breathing in and out deeply like this for several minutes. If your mind wanders, simply notice it, without judgment, then refocus on your breath.

7. As you end the meditation, take note of any changes to your mind, body, and emotions. Note whether you feel calm and relaxed or if any tension or resistance is still hanging around.

TIP: This exercise is not simply about feeling relaxed. You may not always feel more relaxed after a breathing or meditation practice. The purpose is to allow yourself time to observe, without judgment or criticism. This practice will likely help calm you, but it may make you more aware of negative emotions, which can be uncomfortable. Remember, this information is helpful even if it doesn't feel so great!

Recognize It in Your Body

Because emotions are deeply intertwined with our bodies' survival response, it's important that we notice where emotions show up in our bodies. Your body is constantly sending clues about what's going on internally and externally, and it uses emotions as one source of information. Noticing what we're feeling in our body can be the first step to allowing ourselves to identify our automatic thoughts and the emotions that might trigger our inner critic.

Think about a strong emotion that tends to trigger your inner critic. When you're feeling a big wave of this emotion, where do you usually feel it in your body? You may feel different sensations in different parts of your body. For example, when you experience anger, you may feel a tightness in your stomach, shortness of breath, or become flushed or sweaty.

Draw this emotion on the figure on the opposite page. Remember, your drawing doesn't have to be a masterpiece. This is just meant to help you get a sense of where in your body to focus when you feel this triggering emotion. Feel free to keep your drawing simple, or use different colors and shapes to identify different types of sensations in the body.

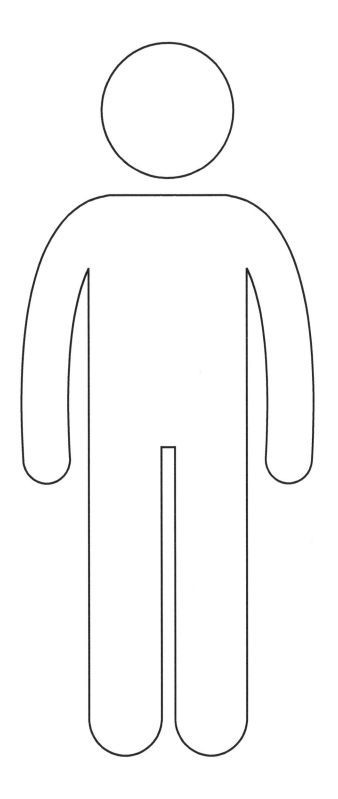

Self-Soothing Touch

Our bodies not only give us information; they can also be one of the most powerful ways for us to practice self-compassion. Biologically, we are wired for touch. Research has found that comforting touch relieves stress, creates a sense of safety, and releases oxytocin (a hormone that produces feelings of love and connection). This is true when we offer it to ourselves as well.

1. Start by placing one hand on top of the other.

2. Notice the warmth and weight of the hand that's on top.

3. Imagine sending warmth and loving-kindness from one hand to the other.

4. Imagine these feelings flowing through your hands and into the rest of your body. Allow them to soothe any tension or emotional distress you might be feeling.

If it's comfortable, try other positions with your hands, moving slowly to a new position when you feel ready:

- Hold or clasp your hands together, perhaps intertwining your fingers.

- Place your hands on your thighs.

- Place one hand on the opposite arm.

- Place one or both hands over your heart.

- Hug yourself by wrapping your arms around you. One way to do this is by placing one hand under the opposite armpit and the other hand on the opposite arm or shoulder.

TIP: Some people feel a lot of discomfort with this kind of touch. I've designed this exercise to give you choices, to see what works best for you. I encourage you to sit with each position as you feel ready, accepting that there may be some discomfort at first. However, if something is too uncomfortable or painful, it's okay to leave it for now and come back later. If you have any kind of trauma that is triggered by physical touch, feel free to skip this exercise or check in with your therapist before trying it.

EMOTIONS ON THE JOB

Sam lost her mother to cancer several months ago. When she's at work and gets a whiff of a chicken casserole someone brought in for the meeting potluck, she gets teary-eyed because it was one of her mom's favorite meals. Suddenly, she has a lump in her throat and feels like curling into a ball in her office. "Just stop it," she thinks to herself. "It's just a casserole. Pull yourself together. Don't be weak. Get back to work."

Curtis is a skilled nurse at a busy hospital. He loves his work and takes pride in being very good at what he does. Part of that involves remaining calm and helpful when patients are severely ill or even when they pass away. When he has an especially hard day at work and ends up crying in the bathroom, he begins to question if he has what it takes to be a nurse.

Sam and Curtis are both experiencing sadness and grief while at work. We often view work as an unemotional place, and when we're feeling emotional, we may worry about expressing those feelings in the workplace. Our concern may be that if we tap into our emotions too much, we'll open a floodgate and be unable to control ourselves. Or we may fear that our coworkers or boss might see us as weak or unprofessional.

The emotional parts of our humanity don't get left at the door when we enter our workplace. For most of us, our job doesn't feel like the safest place for feeling or showing emotion. However, it's still possible to use compassion for ourselves and our emotions while at work—recognizing that we might need some extra TLC once we're off the clock—without criticizing or ignoring our feelings altogether. It's being aware of and understanding our emotions, not ignoring or denying them, that leads to professionalism and healthy functioning.

Loving-Kindness for Your Emotions

You practiced loving-kindness with your thoughts in part 2. Now you can focus on what it means to show up with loving-kindness for your emotions.

1. Using the tools of breath and soothing touch, create a safe, mindful space to repeat this loving-kindness mantra to yourself. Use this time to practice what you've learned so far and notice what feels most helpful to you.

2. You might place your hand on your heart and take a few deep breaths or start with the Breathe into It exercise (page 59), ending with the mantra below.

3. If possible, rather than calling up the feeling of someone else sending you compassion, try to allow yourself to be the source of loving-kindness.

4. You can use your breath or soothing touch as the anchor of your self-compassion practice. Use the warmth and care that you feel as sensations you can come back to when your mind wanders or you notice any discomfort.

5. Repeat this loving-kindness mantra three to five times:

    > May I give myself permission to feel.
    > May I allow space for uncomfortable emotions.
    > May I thank my emotions and body for giving me the information I need.
    > May I allow myself to be soothed by breath and touch.
    > May I accept my emotions as they are.
    > May I accept myself as I am.

Take a moment to reflect on this exercise and write about how it felt to combine different emotional self-compassion skills. What felt most helpful? What would you like to integrate into a daily practice?

Notice the Difference: Self-Critical Response vs. Self-Compassionate Response

Delia is an aspiring musician and is excited to play her first full set at a local bar. However, right before she's due on stage, she begins to feel incredibly nervous. She feels nauseated and begins to get teary-eyed. She bolts outside the bar to get some fresh air. She's running late and can see through the window that the bar staff is looking for her.

Self-Critical Response

Think about how Delia's inner critic might respond to her intense wave of emotion before going on stage. Write that response here.

> *Example: You're so weak. If you get nervous before every gig, you'll never be a real musician.*

....

....

....

How might Delia's inner critic affect her emotional response to this experience?

....

....

....

Self-Compassionate Response

Now write a self-compassionate response to Delia's emotional experience. Include some practices she might use from the previous exercises to show compassion for her emotions.

Example: This is your first gig like this. It's normal to be nervous. Take a few deep breaths, breathing compassion in and tension out.

....

....

....

How might a self-compassionate response affect Delia's emotional reaction to this experience?

....

....

....

The Benefits of Emotional Self-Compassion

Much of the pain I see in my clients is rooted in a denial of their emotional experiences. When we judge our emotions, we naturally end up judging ourselves. Before I learned about self-compassion, I would often tie myself in knots trying to force myself to have the "right" emotion or criticizing myself for having the "wrong" emotion. If emotions were facts, mine appeared to prove that I was weak, ridiculous, and always getting things wrong.

Of course, my family and friends would have had very different things to say about those beliefs, but as I was stuck in my own self-criticism, that didn't matter much. Without self-compassion, I am more likely to lash out at those closest to me. When I'm already in self-criticism about an emotion, it becomes easy to read any response from a loved one as proof that my own judgment is correct, that I'm somehow irrational or inadequate for having such an emotion.

As I learned to be more accepting of myself and my emotions, my emotional life began to shift. I was able to uncoil myself from the distressing cycle of judging myself for very natural emotions. Supporting myself in a moment of distress rather than beating myself up for it was incredibly powerful. I then became more skilled at identifying my emotions and their triggers, understanding what I need and communicating that need accordingly.

I'm not the only one who's benefited from a self-compassion practice. I've seen others find immense healing through self-compassion. Research shows that it is effective in helping us cope with incredibly difficult emotional experiences, including stress, loss, trauma, and chronic physical pain. Self-compassion also aids in our ability to be empathetic with others and helps build our emotional intelligence. Empathy requires that we label emotions, understand emotional experiences, and place ourselves in someone else's emotional landscape. The more compassion and understanding we have for ourselves, the more naturally we can extend it to others.

When we're able to show up for ourselves as a much-needed friend in times of emotional difficulty, we eliminate the battle with our inner critic, opening up new opportunities for deep self-awareness and understanding.

PART FOUR

Self-Compassion in Action

How do we offer compassion to ourselves when we've made a mistake or hurt someone? How do we integrate self-compassion into how we behave and treat ourselves? This section will explore just that—putting self-compassion into action.

Loving You

Beyond your own thoughts and emotions, you might be wondering, "What happens when I mess up in a big way, like when I hurt someone or make a mistake and have to face up to negative consequences? How can I deal with those realities and be self-compassionate without feeling like I'm just making excuses?"

Self-compassion allows us to show up for ourselves in these difficult situations as a supportive partner rather than an internal enemy. Your self-critic may say something like, "I can't believe you! You did this horrible thing, so you must be a horrible person." In contrast, self-compassion says, "Wow, this is a difficult situation for you to deal with. You did something that is out of alignment with who you are. What support do you need in order to act in a way that better matches with what you believe is right?"

On the surface, beating ourselves up may seem like a good motivator, but if we believe we're intrinsically bad, it's much harder for us to believe that we can act differently. It also makes it difficult to show up for others because taking responsibility or asking forgiveness means we have to debase ourselves. Believing we're intrinsically bad makes it harder to face our mistakes and problems while also leading us to become more self-involved. But if we see our screwups and mistakes as behaviors that don't align with our true self, we can more easily grasp the motivation to act differently. We can face others we've hurt knowing that making mistakes is part of relationships and the human experience. Messing up, owning up to it, and trying to make it right is something we're all "meant" to do in our lives.

Our inner critic's message that we are bad if we do something bad can also make us more likely to beat ourselves up mentally and emotionally and engage in self-punishing behaviors. Maybe you tell yourself you're overreacting and too emotional, so you don't reach out to friends for support or you don't allow yourself to take a break and care for your body. You might overeat or impulsively watch TV for hours to numb the pain rather than feel the emotion. Perhaps your inner critic beats you up for not having the perfect body (whatever that is!), which may then lead to denying yourself needed meals, pushing yourself too far on a run (leading to an injury), or not allowing yourself to wear your favorite style of clothing. People who experience clinical depression, anxiety, eating disorders, and self-harm behaviors typically have strong inner critics. But the truth is, whether or not we experience these conditions, many of us have robust inner critics. Either way, self-criticism and shame leave us in the dark, leading us to believe that we don't deserve the very light and the tools we need to find our way.

This doesn't mean we should be harsh to ourselves or our inner critic, though. Meeting our inner critic with self-compassion is the most helpful way to cope with it in the long term.

When I first learned about self-compassion and saw the hurtful impact my inner critic had on my life, I called it names and told it to shut up. I thought if I did that enough, perhaps the self-critic would eventually disappear, or at least become quieter. However, it actually grew louder and more defensive. Once I identified that the deeper motivation of my inner critic was to protect me, I could respond and relate to it with compassion and understanding instead. I might say, "Hey, I know you're trying to protect me. I appreciate that. But I'll take it from here." At that point, I could use the more self-compassionate responses I had learned instead of getting stuck in an internal battle with myself.

We can never fully rid ourselves of self-critical thinking. These thoughts may still come up from time to time—some days more than others. But what we can do is build resiliency through healthy coping tools, like the exercises laid out in this book, which can limit the damage the critic can do. We can find ways to build a self-compassion practice with our thoughts, emotions, and actions that can resist the shaming inner critic.

The exercises in this section will focus on how self-compassion relates to our actions in three ways: how to have self-compassion for our own actions, how to act self-compassionately toward ourselves, and how to put self-compassion into action by integrating our thoughts, emotions, and behaviors.

Forgiving Yourself

When you've done something that hurts others or is out of line with your values, it's important to hold yourself accountable and take responsibility, doing what you can to mend the situation. But holding on to endless guilt and shame only hurts us in the long run and makes it difficult to be our best selves moving forward.

Write about an action that you regret or that felt inconsistent with your values.

....

....

....

....

What makes it hard to forgive yourself for this action? Did you hurt someone? Were there difficult consequences for you?

....

....

....

....

Is there anything you can do to address your resistance to self-forgiveness? Would it help to take responsibility and ask for forgiveness from the person you hurt? Is there a way to solve a problem caused by the negative consequences of your action? Focus on what would be helpful to do next in the situation as it is now, rather than beating yourself up for a past action that you can't change.

....

....

....

....

Before and after the step(s) you identified in the previous question, it can be helpful to show compassion for yourself regarding any feelings of remorse, regret, or pain, as well as the difficulty in facing your mistakes.

Example: This feeling of remorse is painful. We all make mistakes, but it's still so hard to confront the person I hurt.

....

....

....

....

....

The practice of self-compassion leads us to ask ourselves what we need in order to face difficulty. How can you be kind to yourself? What would help you take action to confront the situation and make it right? What would help you give yourself permission to console yourself? If this is hard to identify, think about what you might say or do for a dear friend in the same situation.

Example: I can be kind to myself by journaling and listening to music to process the situation before I talk to the person I hurt.

Who's the Boss?

One of the biggest questions many of us struggle with is, where's the line between having compassion for myself and just making excuses? To help illustrate the benefits of self-compassionate thinking and how it's different from self-indulgence, let's compare a critical boss to a compassionate boss.

With an overly critical and negative boss, you likely don't look forward to the day and feel less confident in your work. Even if you are motivated to do well, it's more likely out of fear, fear of the potential criticism that you'll face if you don't get things right. You may feel more like a hamster on a wheel than a person doing your best.

A compassionate boss will lead you to feel more seen as a person and more confident in your abilities. You will likely be motivated by your enjoyment of the work, your commitment to work well with your team, or the intrinsic value of doing good work. A compassionate boss isn't necessarily a pushover. They hold you accountable without being a jerk about it. It's the same with our self-compassionate voice.

Now think about these two different types of bosses, whether you imagine a real person or make someone up, and complete the following table.

	CRITICAL BOSS	COMPASSIONATE BOSS
What is it like to work for this person? Describe any thoughts, feelings, or actions that come to mind.		
How motivated are you when working for this type of boss? Rate your motivation on a scale from 1 to 10 (10 being the most motivated).		
What is it about this boss's style that motivates you? What doesn't work for you?		
How does this boss's style compare to your own inner critic?		

What does this exercise tell you about motivation and accountability when it comes to self-compassion versus self-criticism? Did this exercise change your perspective in any way?

JULIAN'S STORY

Julian had a difficult childhood. His parents were extremely critical, to the point of emotional and verbal abuse at times. He has struggled with depression and a loud inner critic for as long as he can remember. It wasn't until he started seeing a therapist that he realized there was a connection between the messages of his inner critic and the things his parents used to say to him.

Over the years, he's talked with his parents less and less and often ignores their calls because he doesn't want to deal with their harsh criticism. However, he would always beat himself up for not talking to them. His inner critic would say things like, "They never hurt me physically, so how bad can it be? Why am I so weak that I can't just stand up to them? Why does it affect me so much?" It's painful enough that Julian doesn't feel close to his parents or able to talk to them regularly. His self-criticism was an added layer of pain.

Through working with his therapist and learning how to show himself more compassion, Julian now recognizes that his reluctance to talk to his parents is his way of beginning to set the boundaries he needs. His self-compassion practice reminds him, "These are really hard things to hear. It's okay if I need to draw a line with them. I'm still learning to be kind to myself, and I need time."

It's unlikely that Julian will have an ideal relationship with his parents, but he can start to heal by learning to have the compassion for himself that he rarely felt growing up and by understanding the boundaries he needs to feel safe. As these skills grow stronger, Julian may be able to talk more openly with his parents or adjust his boundaries further. Either way, Julian is working toward being an ally for himself, rather than another critical voice.

Values over Perfection

Our self-critic is often trying to find clear ways to measure whether we're good enough in our lives, work, school, and relationships. We want certainty that we're doing the right thing. However, life is full of unknowns, and the hardest decisions rarely have one clear right answer. If that's the case, what guides us to make decisions and find meaning in life? What do we ground ourselves in when we feel our self-critic coming on strong about making a mistake, acting in a wrong way, or not doing or being enough?

The answer is in our personal core values. Your values guide you without boxing you into perfectionism, which expects you to walk in an exact straight line. Values allow a wider path. There will be twists, turns, mistakes, and off-roading, but your values can guide you toward what's most important to you.

What does your inner critic or perfectionist voice expect from you? What do you end up spending a lot of time doing or worrying about when this voice is loudest?

_____

_____

_____

_____

_____

How do you want to be remembered? When you get to the end of your life, what would you want to stand out as an expression of how you lived your life? If you lived your ideal life, what would matter most to you? What would you spend most of your time doing? Who would you spend your time with? What would give your life meaning?

What overall values can you identify based on what you wrote for the previous question? How do these differ from what you end up focusing on when you're listening to your perfectionism or your inner critic?

Examples: integrity, honesty, love, family, creativity, joy, fun, discipline, gratitude

....

....

....

....

....

Do these values change anything for your now? How does self-compassion come into play when you think about your overall values?

....

....

....

....

....

TIP: Check the Resources section at the back of this book for more exercises to help you identify your specific core values. If you notice any self-judgment come up about a gap between your values and your current actions, practice self-compassion. Remember, compassion is more motivating than fear. You can see this as a check-in or tune-up to nudge yourself back to what's most important rather than a judgment of how poorly you're doing.

Meeting Your Needs with Compassion

Self-compassionate thoughts and emotions lead to self-compassionate actions, such as recognizing and meeting our own needs in real time. The inner critic might tell us that meeting our needs is selfish, so we may let ourselves go without rest, self-care, understanding, or enjoyment, and then we wonder why we're so miserable and irritable. Self-compassion helps us understand what we need in order to remain healthy and engaged with life, from the most basic needs to the most complex ones. It's also much easier to stay mindful of our thoughts and emotions and to practice self-compassion when our basic needs are met.

Use the prompts below to identify and write down your self-care needs. Use the questions and fill-in-the-blank writing prompts in each section to help if you're feeling stuck.

Routine Self-Care

I feel my best when I routinely practice these self-care behaviors:

Examples: adequate sleep, exercise, hygiene routine, reaching out to loved ones, meditation, time outside, saying "no," setting boundaries, time for reflection

....

....

....

....

I can think more clearly if I routinely ....

....

I can manage difficult emotions more readily on days when I _____

_____

I feel my best when I prioritize _____

_____

Red Flags

These behaviors are clues that I'm punishing myself or neglecting my needs:

Examples: overextending or overscheduling myself, lack of adequate sleep, over/undereating, not prioritizing time for myself, obsessing over mistakes

_____

_____

_____

_____

The first self-care behaviors that I let go of when I'm struggling are

_____

I'm most irritable when I _____

_____

When my self-critic gets really loud, I tend to _____

_____

First Steps

These are things I can do to get back on track when I notice I've lost my way:

_____

_____

_____

_____

Self-care behaviors I view as a special treat or boost: _____

_____

A supportive person I can reach out to: _____

_____

One or two simple behaviors that I can start with: _____

_____

TIP: Be realistic and kind even in your identification of a self-care plan. Keep it simple. When you notice your red flags popping up, practice self-compassion and work back to a more helpful routine by gradually implementing one or two self-care behaviors at a time.

Compassionate Boundaries

Some resistance to being kind to ourselves lies in the belief that self-compassion is selfish or indulgent and will keep us from being as mindful of our loved ones' needs. Research debunks this theory. Compassion is not limited—the more there is, the more everyone can feel it and the more it can grow. Setting healthy boundaries for ourselves and with others can be one of the most powerful ways to practice self-compassion.

When you have healthy boundaries, it's okay to

- say "no"

- take needed time for yourself and your self-care

- maintain your personal/physical space

- separate your needs and emotions from those of others

- protect yourself from harmful relationships and situations

- stick to your values

- communicate your needs and emotions openly with those you trust

- maintain your privacy

- have difficult conversations

- take responsibility for your own needs and emotions

Which, if any, of the above components of healthy boundaries seem significant to you? Which do you tend to do easily? (While the list above is helpful, it's not necessarily exhaustive. Feel free to identify other ways you maintain your boundaries.)

....

....

....

....

In what specific ways do you most struggle with boundaries?

Examples: Allowing my partner's mood to dictate my own mood or feeling responsible for changing their mood. Sacrificing quality family time due to working long hours. Blaming my children for the fact that I don't prioritize time for myself anymore.

How does your inner critic play a role in how you set (or don't set) healthy boundaries?

Examples: It tells me it's all my fault if someone is upset or inconvenienced by my boundary. It tells me I'm horrible and selfish if I say "no" to a loved one. It says I'm a failure if I tell my boss I need to extend a deadline.

What would your self-compassionate voice tell you about setting boundaries?

Examples: It's okay to say "no" sometimes. I can't do everything. It's hard to balance competing priorities, and it's okay to need time away when you're struggling with that.

AFFIRMATION

You might notice yourself thinking, "But I can't be kind to myself if I haven't been kind to others!" Take a deep breath and think for a moment about a dear friend, your child, or even yourself as a young child. If any of those people made a mistake or hurt someone, would your care for them evaporate? Would you no longer believe your child or closest friend is worthy of any compassion?

Research shows that even if we don't lessen our levels of self-criticism, developing more self-compassion can lead to better emotional and mental wellbeing. So even if you're still noticing a pretty loud self-critic, practicing self-compassion when you can will help. The better we feel, the more likely we are to act in thoughtful ways that align with what's most important to us. Believe it or not, boundaries, accountability, motivation, and self-compassion all go hand in hand.

Tune In with the Senses

Tapping into our senses is a powerful way to integrate mindfulness and compassion in our daily life. Much like the soothing touch we practiced in part 3, physical sensations create an added layer of comfort and understanding that can make our self-compassion practice more powerful.

For each sense listed below, write down some of the most comforting scents, sounds, or sensations you associate with it.

SENSE	EXAMPLES	WHAT WORKS FOR YOU
Sound	favorite song	
	nature sounds	
	someone's voice	
	silence	
Sight	a specific color	
	reading a book	
	nature scenes	
Smell	flowers	
	specific foods	
	candles	
Taste	a specific food	
	candies	
	a specific beverage	
Touch	a type of soothing touch	
	soft blanket	
	warm bath	

Choose at least one or two of the experiences you identified and make time to create that experience for yourself. Be mindful and pay attention as you do.

Example: Give yourself an extra 5 to 10 minutes to slowly sip your coffee or tea, noticing how it tastes and feels (rather than just gulping it down). Or lie under your favorite soft blanket, noticing its weight on your body, rubbing the soft fibers, feeling its warmth.

Write about the experience(s) below and practical ways you could add soothing sensation into your daily routine or to support you during difficult times.

TIP: This is a great practice to add to a loving-kindness meditation. Practice sending loving-kindness to the source of the soothing sensation (yes, send care and thanks to your blanket, your coffee, or favorite music artist). Then, imagine that source sending loving-kindness to you as you practice really allowing yourself to notice and enjoy the sensations.

Health Values

Cultural standards of beauty become ingrained at a young age, and body image and health issues tend to trigger a lot of self-criticism. This exercise will help you identify how to use values as a guide for compassionate action rather than self-judgment. You can answer these questions in terms of body image, chronic illness or disability, or any other health or body matters.

TIP: If you experience disordered eating or have physical, medical, or other trauma that affects your self-criticism related to your body, it may be helpful to first discuss this exercise with your therapist or trusted health professional.

Does your inner critic show up in regard to your body or health? If so, what are some of its most common messages?

Examples: You'll never be thin enough. You're such a slob. You're so weak when you let your chronic illness affect you this way.

Do these messages cause you to punish or neglect yourself or your body? If so, in what ways?

Examples: Over/undereating, yo-yo dieting, exercising to the point of injury, not seeking medical attention when needed

What does your body/health provide for you now, even if it doesn't meet your inner critic's standards?

Examples: My body moves me through the world so that I can work, be with family, exercise, etc. My body and brain work together to keep me breathing and alive each day.

....

....

....

What are more realistic and compassionate ways of relating to your body or health?

Examples: I can't expect myself to have the body of an elite athlete when that's not my full-time job. I can eat nutritiously without punishing myself for having a treat.

....

....

....

How could identifying an overall health value lead to more compassionate action?

Example: Rather than having the perfect body, my value is to nourish my body. I can eat foods and engage in exercise that support my body in a sustainable way, rather than punish my body for not being perfect.

....

....

....

Empathizing with the Inner Critic

We've talked a lot about your inner critic and how listening to its messages can be detrimental. However, using its own tactics against it isn't very effective. As we discussed in part 3, the self-critic is often motivated by the survival response. Its deepest desire is to protect you, even if it doesn't do that very well. Being critical of the inner critic typically just elicits more fear and defensiveness. Just as we set boundaries with other people, we can hold limits with the inner critic while still empathizing with its fear and worry.

Call up your inner critic for a moment. Imagine the tone of its voice, its go-to sayings, its best tactics, and its biggest fears. You might imagine that your inner critic is similar to a person in your life, a character in a movie, a version of you, or an imaginary creature. Use the space on the next page to draw a picture of your inner critic. Keep its fears in mind, and include in your drawing some of the ways it tries to protect and defend itself.

Remember, this doesn't need to be a masterpiece. Drawing can be a helpful way to better understand abstract concepts. Use the questions on pages 95–96 to inform your drawing.

What more did you learn about your inner critic by drawing it? Does imagining it this way change how you relate to it?

What is its deepest fear behind the criticism? What is it most scared of?

What is its ultimate goal?

How do your inner critic's fears and goals relate to your own?

How might you show empathy and self-compassion to this part of yourself, the fearful, protective inner critic? How might showing self-compassion change the way that you interact with your inner critic?

CYNTHIA'S STORY

Cynthia has struggled with her body image for as long as she can remember. She's always trying the next diet or workout routine, hoping it will be "the one." If she could just lose those 10 pounds, everything would be different.

Cynthia's been cycling through the same pattern for years. She'll try a new diet, really limit her calories, or start a new intense workout regimen, and she'll lose a little weight. But eventually, the caloric deficit is too much, or she'll go on a trip, which interrupts her routine. Every time this happens, Cynthia berates herself, "You're such a fat slob. You'll never be thin enough. You'll never have the discipline you need." This self-criticism makes her feel worse and leads her to try to numb her pain through overeating, undereating, or neglecting exercise. It's an emotional and physical roller coaster.

One day, Cynthia looks back at photos from a few years before. She believes she weighed 20 pounds less then. But looking back, she remembers having the same thoughts and feelings about her body that she has now. No matter the number on the scale, she has always judged her eating, exercise, and weight. It's never good enough.

What if Cynthia could see her body and her health in a different way? Instead of chasing the perfect body or health regimen (and, ultimately, punishing and neglecting herself in the process), she might work toward identifying long-term health values that are more sustainable. Rather than forms of measurement and punishment, Cynthia could look at food and exercise as tools for nourishing her body and feeling good. Valuing nourishment can lead to healthy behaviors that are more sustainable and allow more room for rest, the occasional treat, and compassion when things don't go as planned.

Loving-Kindness for Your Whole Self

Meaningful self-compassion is about understanding and truly caring for the many complex parts of ourselves. It's not about painting a rosy picture or using nice platitudes to put a temporary bandage on our struggles. Acceptance and understanding of our whole selves can lead to true healing.

Beneath the perfectionism, the self-critic, the face you put on for the world, who are you? What are your strengths? What are your flaws and weaknesses?

What about yourself is hard to appreciate when your self-critic is in charge but easier to see through self-compassion?

Using breath, soothing touch, or other mindfulness skills you've learned so far, repeat the loving-kindness mantra below to yourself at least three times.

> May I accept myself as I am:
> Flaws, strengths, complications, and all.
> May I learn to befriend all parts of myself:
> The good, the fearful, the angry, the not-yet.
> May I find compassion for myself,
> Even when I feel hard to love.
> May I offer loving-kindness to my whole self.

Because it's hard to encapsulate something as complex as a whole human self, this is a great opportunity to use creativity. Try one of the ideas below, or create your own.

- Write the loving-kindness mantra (or your own) on a beautiful card or poster that you can look at regularly.

- Create an image through drawing, painting, or collage that encapsulates the idea of accepting your whole self.

- Choose a photo or object that represents your whole self. Journal or reflect on what wholeness means to you.

- Write a self-compassionate letter to yourself, reminding yourself that you are more than your mistakes or weaknesses. Place it somewhere you can refer to often.

Notice the Difference: Self-Critical Response vs. Self-Compassionate Response

Kimaya receives a text asking what time she'll be over tomorrow to help her friend move into a new apartment. Kimaya stops in her tracks, as she realizes she got her dates mixed up and had also committed to attend and help prepare her nephew's birthday party the same day. Kimaya knows her friend needs a lot of help but also values quality family time and celebrations. She feels horrible for making this mistake and having to say no to someone she cares about.

Self-Critical Response

Identify Kimaya's thoughts and emotions that may come up if her inner critic takes over.

Example: You are seriously the worst friend and aunt. You're so sloppy and disorganized. You're a total disappointment!

....

....

....

....

How might Kimaya's self-critical internal response affect her actions?

Example: Kimaya feels so bad that she doesn't tell her friend about the mistake she made. She says she'll be there but doesn't show up.

....

....

....

Self-Compassionate Response

In what ways could Kimaya show herself compassion in response to her mistake and initial remorse?

Example: She might take deep, mindful breaths and say to herself, "You're trying to juggle so much. Scheduling mistakes happen to everyone."

How might self-compassion affect Kimaya's actions in this scenario?

Example: After taking some time to breathe and repeat loving-kindness phrases, Kimaya calls her friend to explain the situation and apologize for the mishap. They find another friend who is able to help with the move so Kimaya can focus on her family event.

The Benefits of Self-Compassionate Behavior

The benefits of self-compassion on our behavior are similar to those we've discussed previously in the book. Our thoughts and emotions obviously have a huge effect on our reactions, so it makes sense that more awareness of our internal world and healthy coping lead to healthier behaviors. A strong self-compassion practice doesn't keep us from making mistakes, but it gives us better tools and understanding to cope with our own errors, flaws, and struggles.

When we have higher levels of mental and emotional well-being, we're able to take better care of ourselves. If we stay stuck in a stress response, dealing with the actual stress of life *plus* our intense self-criticism, we are more likely to react impulsively. When we're able to support ourselves through life's difficulties, we tend to have more capacity for responding in thoughtful ways to others and our environment.

Self-compassion enables us to consider the entire complex, messy picture of who we are as a whole person. The inner critic tends to scold us for making any type of mistake or unwise action, as if being flawed negates all our other strengths and our inherent value. But with self-compassion, we can face the worst parts of ourselves—our greatest weaknesses and screwups in life—while knowing they're only part of the story. This allows us to take responsibility for our own stumbles and imperfections without being cruel to ourselves. Rather than being stuck in an impulsive, defensive reaction to our inner critic, we can take action to find resolution, forgiveness, and a way forward. When we're stuck in the deep shame our inner critic uses, we feel isolated and unworthy, which makes it much harder to face a difficult situation or ask forgiveness from someone we've hurt.

Although our initial reaction to self-compassion may be a fear that we'll be overly indulgent or make excuses for ourselves, the truth is that self-compassion in the long term can motivate us, lead to positive change, and increase our ability to connect with and stay accountable to ourselves and the people in our lives.

PART FIVE

Onward, Upward

Self-compassion is a lifelong practice that develops over time. In this section, you'll reflect on what works best for you and how to practically take what you've learned into your day-to-day life for years to come.

Finding What Works for You

At this point, you've practiced as many as 30 different self-compassion strategies. That's incredible! Take a moment to acknowledge the work you've done so far. Even when it seems simple, none of this work is easy. You have likely pushed through a good amount of doubt and self-criticism. That's normal. Thank yourself for being open to learning something new and willing to show up for yourself in this way.

There are a few things to keep in mind as you begin your new self-compassion practice.

Keep it simple.

There's no need to overcomplicate things. Start small and allow yourself to take your time as you learn this new skill.

Go at your own pace.

Although this book is short, it may take more time than you anticipated to do all the exercises. It's okay to stay on one exercise for a while. For instance, you may practice and reflect on one exercise over the course of a week or longer. There's no reason to rush. Giving yourself time to reflect is incredibly helpful.

Integrate self-compassion into your daily routine.

Practicing daily, even when we're feeling good, is incredibly helpful. Applying self-compassion in neutral times will help it feel more natural when you're really struggling.

Make self-compassion practices part of your current routine. You might add a loving-kindness meditation after your daily workout or practice one self-compassion exercise before bed each night.

Use these skills any time: when you spill coffee on your shirt, when your child falls on the playground, when your dog poops on the neighbor's lawn and you're out of bags, when the store is out of your favorite snack—no struggle is too small.

Make it your own.

Not all of the exercises in this book will be effective for you, and it's okay if you don't try every single one. I certainly don't expect anyone to practice every exercise from this book regularly. Try as many as you can, knowing that it's most important to identify what works best for you. Feel free to modify and add to exercises so that your practice makes the most sense for you.

It's useful to take note of what works best for you as you begin to create your own personal self-compassion habit. Write down a few of the exercises that most resonate with you and what feels most helpful about each one. Include the page number of the exercise so you can easily reference it again later.

Exercise name and page number: _____

It felt helpful because _____

_____

_____

Exercise name and page number: _____

It felt helpful because _____

_____

_____

Exercise name and page number: ....

It felt helpful because ....

....

....

Exercise name and page number: ....

It felt helpful because ....

....

....

Exercise name and page number: ....

It felt helpful because ....

....

....

Take note of one or two exercises that were particularly difficult. Resistance can indicate soft spots that are important to pay attention to, as they can provide further insight into our inner critic. Give yourself permission to be gentle with yourself, and come back to the exercises whenever you're ready.

Exercises I may want to come back to later:

....

....

....

Short-Term Outlook

This workbook is designed to be used over and over to help you build self-compassion skills and develop resiliency to self-criticism, shame, and the inevitable difficulties of life. As you continue strengthening your self-compassion skills, keep the following in mind:

Self-compassion is an ongoing practice, not a project to be completed or perfected.
There is no one right way to integrate self-compassion into your life. Be mindful not to use the exercises in this book as another avenue for perfectionism and self-criticism. Much like yoga or parenting, self-compassion is a living, breathing set of tools that grows and changes with us over time. I've been practicing self-compassion for years, and while my practice continues to deepen, there's always more to learn.

Every day is different. It's normal to feel stuck sometimes.
We all have bad days. Some days, self-compassion will feel more natural than others. Other days you'll worry that you're failing or will never get it right. That doesn't mean you've lost all your progress. You're just having a tough day or week or month. It happens to all of us.

Don't criticize your criticism.
Once you become aware of your inner critic, you will hear it more and more. You might be shocked or overwhelmed by how often your inner critic takes center stage. This heightened awareness typically happens quickly, before you're able to build confidence in the self-compassion tools that make the inner critic's voice less overwhelming. When you notice this happening, have compassion for yourself as you experience this difficult process.

The practice is in the doing.
Knowledge about self-compassion is helpful in many ways. But until we actually see how self-compassion works for us in our day-to-day lives or when struggles set in, it will be hard to fully understand. As you learn what self-compassion looks like in your daily life and in your practice, it might be different than what you initially expected. Taking time to reflect and get creative will help this practice become more natural and personal for you.

Long-Term Outlook

Hopefully, this workbook inspires a self-compassion practice for you that lasts for years to come. Once you've gained the awareness of self-compassion, it's hard to go back.

Growth and healing aren't linear.

We tend to think healthy growth is a straight line, always trending upward. As we experience growth day to day, though, it rarely feels like a steady, stable process. Some days we'll feel like we're making great strides. Other days will feel like we're walking through mud, barely moving, or even like we've regressed and fallen backward. There are always dips, ups and downs, even curlicues, as we work toward deep personal growth. A self-compassion practice is no different.

The biggest part of the practice is simply having the will to show up.

If you can show up to practice today, even if it's feeling particularly hard, that's part of the process. You can acknowledge your courage and persistence in showing up again, especially when it's more difficult. It's okay if you have days, weeks, or months when these self-compassion exercises don't feel as helpful as normal. You won't always feel instant effects from your self-compassion practice, but you'll be thankful you did it, and you'll experience positive changes in the long run.

Growth is easier to see over time.

Be careful to keep your expectations realistic. Change doesn't happen overnight. Although, rationally, we know that, we may still hold ourselves to the expectation that we should be self-compassion masters within a month. But deep, meaningful growth tends to be slow and gradual. It happens at a pace that is hard to see from one day to the next, but over longer periods of time, over years, the growth becomes much more obvious. There will be ups and downs, but over time, you will see growth.

It's okay to go back to the beginning.

Once I notice I've been neglecting my self-compassion practice (and, consequently, my own well-being) for a while, I say to myself, "Just start again. Go back to the compassion." It's not that I'm starting over. The beauty of self-compassion is that it will be there for you even after a long break. The very foundation of self-compassion lies in our ability to support ourselves when we most need it.

You're kind of like an onion.

Often, our growth leads us to discover other places for learning that we couldn't see at first. For instance, you'll peel off one layer of the onion: the very awareness that an inner critic exists and isn't always helpful. Until you can name that layer, you can't see the specific messages of the critic and how they affect you. Rather than seeing new challenges as setbacks, see them as progress. The only way you made it to this challenge is because you did the work on the layer before it.

This also means you may uncover especially painful layers. This pain isn't there because you're practicing self-compassion. It was there all along, but it was masked underneath the many layers of defense the inner critic put in place. You might realize hard truths about your upbringing, deep hurt from a past relationship, or feel knocked sideways from the very act of saying your inner critic's words about yourself out loud. Practice tenderness and care for yourself in these times.

Reach out.

If you notice yourself feeling stuck or uncovering an especially difficult layer, remember that you're not alone. Reach out to a trusted friend or loved one. Consider working with a therapist or counselor if you're feeling especially raw from this work. Hopefully, this book has given you the language and tools to talk with others about your inner critic and self-compassion strategies.

Deepen your practice with other books and resources.

Thankfully, with the growing research and understanding of the benefits of self-compassion and mindfulness, there are tons of resources to grow your practice. The work of researchers like Kristin Neff, Christopher Germer, Brené Brown, Tim Desmond, and Russ Harris (just to name a few) inspired much of this book. Check the Resources section in the back of this book for more information, including books, online courses, retreats, meditation apps, and more.

You've got this!

Self-compassion is a practice that anyone can learn and cultivate. You don't have to be a therapist or guru to feel its benefits. You just have to be willing to give it a try and come back to it each new day. As always, be kind to yourself. Don't compare your practice to others. Wherever you are with your self-compassion practice right now is where you are. Just take the next compassionate step.

My Self-Compassion Care Plan

Use the guide below to create your own self-compassion care plan, a sustainable individualized plan that helps you apply the concepts from the book directly to your life. Fill out the following plan based on what skills and tools from this book you have found the most helpful. You can always change and update it as your practice grows and changes.

Daily reminders, even when we're feeling good or neutral, are incredibly helpful in allowing us to remember self-compassion is an option when we're really struggling. Use exercises from this book or anything else you've noticed to be helpful for you, such as daily self-care activities, setting boundaries, or repeating a mantra every morning.

These daily practices can help me stay mindful and practice self-compassion regularly:

_____

_____

_____

_____

List any thoughts, emotions, body sensations, and behaviors that are red flags for your inner critic.

_____

_____

_____

_____

_____

List any of the exercises in this book or other strategies that work for you, such as the breathing or mindfulness exercises, giving yourself permission, the soothing touch or sense exercises, or thinking about what you'd say to a friend.

When my inner critic gets loud, these are most helpful ways to remind myself of self-compassion in the moment:

Knowing who you can trust to support your self-compassion practice is helpful. We don't need to go it alone.

I can reach out to these supportive people when I'm struggling:

You can use any of the loving-kindness or mantra exercises from this book or from a song, poem, or another book or a personal phrase that you like.

My personal self-compassion mantra is:

Identify your values and goals as reminders of why you want to keep doing this work. Keeping up a daily practice isn't always easy, so knowing why we want to do it is helpful.

My self-compassion practice is important to me because:

_____

_____

_____

_____

There will always be room for growth, but that doesn't mean you have to tackle it all right now. Take note of what you'd like to work toward, while giving yourself time, space, and compassion to integrate what you're just learning.

I want to continue to explore and expand these areas of growth in my self-compassion practice in the future:

_____

_____

_____

_____

_____

Resources

Websites

Compassion

Brené Brown and the Daring Way: BreneBrown.com/TheDaringWay

As a certified Daring Way facilitator, I find Brené Brown's research on shame and vulnerability incredibly helpful to understanding our inner critic. Here, you can find a group or therapist in your area that can help you better understand your inner critic and how to build further self-compassion and resiliency.

Center for Mindful Self-Compassion: CenterForMSC.org

Run by leading researchers of self-compassion, this website provides access to online courses, support groups, trainings, and retreats to help you deepen your practice.

Self-Compassion.org: Self-Compassion.org

This is the website of Kristin Neff, one of the leading researchers in self-compassion. Here you'll find further resources from Neff's work, including more exercises, meditations, and research articles.

Self-Compassion Scale by Kristin Neff: Self-Compassion.org/test-how-self -compassionate-you-are

This research-based measurement scale is designed to help you measure your compassion. It breaks your score down to measure different components of self-compassion and can be helpful in learning where to focus your practice.

Mindful Movement

LifeForce Yoga: YogaForDepression.com

This evidence-based protocol for mood regulation through yoga was developed by Amy Weintraub. The website includes videos, books, classes, and workshops.

Yoga with Adriene: YogaWithAdriene.com

This website offers hundreds of free, accessible yoga videos. Adriene has a down-to-earth style and encourages you to have compassion and awareness in your practice rather than pushing yourself to get the poses just right.

Mindfulness and Meditation

Calm.com

This website and app offers guided meditations to build your mindfulness skills.

Mindful.org and **MindfulDirectory.org**

This non-profit offers a directory of events and mindfulness teachers, as well as a magazine and countless online articles written by professionals. Many articles offer free guided meditations and other insights related to building mindful self-compassion.

"The RAIN of Self-Compassion" by Tara Brach: TaraBrach.com/the-rain-of -self-compassion

This discussion and accompanying meditation practice will help you learn self-compassion and understand how to avoid "the suffering of being at war with ourselves."

Self-Compassion Meditations by Christopher Germer: ChrisGermer.com/meditations

These free recorded meditations and mindfulness practices were created by one of the leading researchers on self-compassion.

Street Lovingkindness Video Series by Sharon Salzberg: SharonSalzberg.com/street-lovingkindness-video-series

This series on practically applying loving-kindness to daily life was created by one of the leading meditation teachers and authors on this practice.

UMass Memorial Center for Mindfulness: UMassMemorialHealthcare.org/umass-memorial-center-mindfulness

Founded by Jon Kabat-Zinn, this leading institution in mindfulness-based stress reduction (MBSR) offers online classes, courses, and trainings.

Values

Values Cards Exercise: Think2Perform.com/our-approach/values

This is a helpful exercise in identifying your personal core values. Knowing your core values can help when your inner critic/perfectionist makes things murky and you need to redirect.

The Values Cards: QCards.com.au/the-values-cards

You can purchase a physical card deck here to explore your values. It offers several methods to help you determine your core values. You can also purchase downloadable PDF versions of the deck and instructions.

Books

The Gifts of Imperfection: Let Go of Who You Think You're Supposed to Be and Embrace Who You Are by Brené Brown

Lovingkindness: The Revolutionary Art of Happiness by Sharon Salzberg

The Mindful Path to Self-Compassion: Freeing Yourself from Destructive Thoughts and Emotions by Christopher Germer

The Self-Compassion Deck: 50 Mindfulness Based Practices (card deck) by Mitch Abblett, Tim Desmond, and Christopher Willard

Self-Compassion: The Proven Power of Being Kind to Yourself by Kristin Neff

References

Ackerman, Courtney E. "Cognitive Distortions: When Your Brain Lies to You." PositivePsychology.com. April 15, 2020. positivepsychology.com/cognitive-distortions.

Brown, Brené. *Daring Greatly: How the Courage to Be Vulnerable Transforms the Way We Live, Love, Parent, and Lead.* New York: Avery, 2015.

David, Susan. "3 Ways to Better Understand Your Emotions." *Harvard Business Review.* November 10, 2016. hbr.org/2016/11/3-ways-to-better-understand-your-emotions.

Desmond, Tim. *The Self-Compassion Skills Workbook: A 14-Day Plan to Transform Your Relationship with Yourself.* New York: W. W. Norton, 2017.

Harris, Russ. *ACT Made Simple: An Easy-To-Read Primer on Acceptance and Commitment Therapy.* Oakland, CA: New Harbinger Publications, 2019.

Harris, Russ. *The Happiness Trap: How to Stop Struggling and Start Living.* Boston: Shambala Publications, 2008.

Kolts, Russell. "Bringing Compassion to Anger." Awareness in Action. January 7, 2020. awarenessinaction.org/bringing-compassion-to-anger.

Merriam-Webster. S.v. "loving-kindness." Accessed May 24, 2020. merriam-webster.com/dictionary/loving-kindness.

Neff, Kristin, and Christopher Germer. *The Mindful Self-Compassion Workbook: A Proven Way to Accept Yourself, Build Inner Strength, and Thrive.* New York: Guilford Press, 2018.

Neff, Kristin, and Katie A. Dahm. "Self-Compassion: What It Is, What It Does, and How It Relates to Mindfulness." Accessed April 13, 2020. self-compassion.org/wp-content/uploads/publications/Mindfulness_and_SC_chapter_in_press.pdf.

Neff, Kristin. *Self-Compassion: The Proven Power of Being Kind to Yourself*. London: Hodder & Stoughton, 2013.

Raes, Filip, Elizabeth Pommier, Kristin D. Neff, and Dinska Van Gucht. "Construction and Factorial Validation of a Short Form of the Self-Compassion Scale." *Clinical Psychology & Psychotherapy* 18 (2011): 250–55. doi.org/10.1002/cpp.702.

Schwartz, Richard. "Using Internal Family Systems to Reduce Self-Criticism." *Psychotherapy Networker*. psychotherapynetworker.org/blog/details/634 /using-internal-family-systems-to-reduce-self-criticism.

Acknowledgments

To my husband, Travis, thank you for always believing in me and providing much-needed encouragement throughout the process of writing this book.

To Alison Harney and our Artist's Way writing group in Atlanta, thanks for helping me get creatively "unblocked." Joining this group right before starting this book was the perfect example of creative serendipity.

To every supervisor, mentor, colleague, and client I've had in my career, a simple "thanks" is not enough. You have brought meaning and learning to my life in a way I could never quantify!

The research and work of Kristin Neff, Brené Brown, Christopher Germer, Tim Desmond, Russ Harris, and many others greatly inspired my writing this book and my therapeutic work. Your commitment to providing research that allows for evidence-based care is invaluable.

To the team at Callisto Media and my kind, compassionate editor, Crystal Nero, thank you for believing in me and putting everything in motion to make this book happen.

About the Author

 Joy Johnson is a licensed clinical social worker and psychotherapist in Atlanta, Georgia. Her work as a psychotherapist, and writer, is aimed at helping hard-working people who take care of everything and everyone else learn to take care of themselves and avoid burnout. Joy identifies as one of those people, and she first discovered self-compassion as a powerful personal practice to navigate her own struggles. Her passion for this work is rooted in the powerful healing it has brought to her life and the lives of her clients.

Joy received her master's degree in social work from the University of North Carolina at Chapel Hill and has extensive experience in the field of mental health.

Learn more about her work at Joy-Johnson.com and TherapyWithJoy.com